T0060645

HOW TO DO THE RIGHT THING

ANCIENT WISDOM FOR MODERN READERS

■ ■ ■ ■

HOW TO DO
THE RIGHT THING

■ ■ ■ ■ ■ ■

An Ancient Guide to Treating People Fairly

Seneca

Selected, translated, and introduced
by Robert A. Kaster

PRINCETON UNIVERSITY PRESS

PRINCETON AND OXFORD

Published by Princeton University Press
41 William Street, Princeton, New Jersey 08540
99 Banbury Road, Oxford OX2 6JX

press.princeton.edu

All Rights Reserved

ISBN 9780691238647
ISBN (e-book) 9780691238654

British Library Cataloging-in-Publication Data is available

Editorial: Rob Tempio and Chloe Coy
Production Editorial: Mark Bellis
Text Design: Pamela Schnitter
Jacket Design: Heather Hansen
Production: Erin Suydam
Publicity: Alyssa Sanford and Carmen Jimenez
Copyeditor: Kathleen Kageff

Jacket Credit: *Justice* by Antonio Canova, 1792. Milan /
Gallerie di Piazza Scala

This book has been composed in Stempel Garamond LT Std
with Futura Std

Printed on acid-free paper. ∞

Printed in the United States of America

1 3 5 7 9 10 8 6 4 2

CONTENTS

INTRODUCTION

"That's not fair!"

I cannot now recall how old my two children were when those familiar words first passed their lips, but it was probably somewhere in the mid-single digits. Though I recall being a bit surprised the first time around, I shouldn't have been. The exclamation seems to emerge from a primal human sense: you know how you deserve to be treated, and you know that, just now, you have not been treated that way—you've been given a raw deal; you've not been done right by. That is the sense of fairness this book explores—fairness at the everyday, person-to-person level—taking as its source

the ethical writings of the Stoic philosopher and Roman statesman Seneca.

Born near the end of the first century BCE or very early in the new era, to an Italian family that had settled in southern Spain, Seneca was educated in literature, rhetoric, and philosophy in Rome. He lived quietly and (from our vantage point) obscurely, in Rome and for a time in Egypt, until he began a career as a minor magistrate and senator sometime in the 30s CE, after a well-connected aunt pulled some strings. But in 41 his comfortable way of life blew up, as the emperor Claudius sent him into exile for committing adultery with a sister of Claudius's predecessor, the psychopath Caligula.

For eight years he lived in isolation on Corsica—then one of the wildest, roughest

places in the Mediterranean—until Agrippina, Claudius's new wife, prevailed on him to recall Seneca so that he could supervise the education of her son, the twelve-year-old Nero. The association set the course for the rest of Seneca's life. When Nero was adopted by Claudius in 50 and soon became the heir apparent, Seneca was still his tutor. When Nero became emperor in 54, Seneca became one of his chief advisers. When Nero had his mother murdered in 59, Seneca stood by him, drafting a letter—a cover-up that fooled no one—for Nero to send to the Senate. In 62, as Nero was becoming ever more erratic and proximity to him ever more dangerous, Seneca formally requested permission to retire and, when permission was not granted, informally withdrew from court. And in 65, when a conspiracy to assassinate the

emperor was detected and its members punished, Seneca was falsely implicated and forced to commit suicide.

And throughout all that time—in fact, starting under Caligula, before his exile—Seneca was compiling a vast output of poetry and prose, much of which survives today as the most diverse and influential body of literature produced by a Roman writer in the first century of our era. His prose writings are largely devoted to ethics and treat a great range of topics from a predominantly Stoic point of view. These texts provide the raw material for our consideration of everyday fair dealings between ordinary people: for though that sense of fairness is not the central topic in any of Seneca's ethical writings, principles and

words of advice relevant to the virtue's practice appear throughout them.

The excerpts that make up this book are drawn from three different collections:[1]

- two works, *On Benefits* and *On Mercy*, were transmitted together from antiquity, presumably because they are both concerned with forms of "giving": the first devotes seven books to ethical and practical guidelines for dispensing and repaying favors; the second urges Nero to take a clement approach in dispensing punishments;[2]
- ten essays written at various times on disparate themes are collected under the title *Dialogues:* for our purposes, the essay *On Anger*, a meditation on the dangers of rage in three books, is the

most substantial and most important; excerpts are also drawn from the essays *On Tranquility of Mind*, *On the Happy Life*, and *On the Consistency of the Wise*;

- the most influential of these works, the *Moral Epistles*, is a collection of over 120 letters written after Seneca's withdrawal from public life, all addressed to his slightly younger friend Lucilius, as he traces their attempt to make progress on the journey toward wisdom.

The passages chosen from these works are organized in five chapters, and while each chapter gives a different view of what fair dealing demands—"Striving for Magnanimity," "Being Calm, Thinking Clearly," "Judging Yourself Fairly," "Doing Right by Others," and "Being Merciful"—they are all unified by the predominantly Stoic point

of view that Seneca favors. Some details of that viewpoint will be explained as they become relevant to our progress in the chapters that follow, but it should be useful to set out briefly here some of the Stoics' key beliefs and premises.

The universe is everywhere pervaded by a beneficent and providential God, which the Stoics also called "nature" or "reason." God shaped the universe and set it in motion in such a way that all living creatures are able to flourish within it, and for all living creatures, save one sort, that flourishing—the final good that they instinctively seek—is physical well-being: nourishment, shelter, reproduction, and the rest. The exceptional sort is the category consisting of human beings, who are exceptional in two ways: they alone have a share in the divine reason that governs the universe, and because of

that share they alone cannot consider physical well-being to be their final good.

For human beings, the final good is virtue—for us, only "virtue" provides a valid subject for the predicate "is a good thing for me," just as only "the absence of virtue" is a valid subject of the predicate "is a bad thing for me"—and virtue is one thing, and one thing only, a unified whole: it is the mind's consistent and unceasing exercise of reason, as it makes true judgments and right choices in every circumstance. Individual traits that we call "virtues"—like courage and fidelity and, yes, fairness—are only the actions of the rational mind making true judgments and right choices in particular circumstances.[3]

Living the best human life, the Stoics say, consists of "living according to nature," by which they mean exercising to the full the

capacities with which nature—the providential God who orders the universe—
equipped us. Only in that way can we enjoy
the one good that is an end in itself, worthy
of being sought for its own sake. All things
external to the rational mind that are commonly labeled "good" or "bad"—health,
wealth, and power, or sickness, poverty, and
oppression—do not contribute to or detract
from the best human life: they are merely
"indifferent." We can legitimately prefer to
have some of these "indifferents," like good
health, and prefer not to have others, like
sickness, and we can legitimately seek the
former and try to avoid the latter—if and
only if we do not seek them as ends in
themselves or shun them as things that are
truly bad.

(And if you have read the preceding three
paragraphs with frank disbelief, know that

most or all of the good advice that follows can be accepted and found helpful without signing on to the premises I've described.)

So, yes, to say the least, it is an austere doctrine (though not, as we'll see, a cold- or stone-hearted one), and we can understand why those who deserve to be called "wise" according to the standard it sets—those who have learned to live entirely "according to nature"—are at most exceedingly rare. But for the warmly human virtue that is the topic of this book, we can also understand why a Stoic would think that you cannot be fair and do right by others unless you sort yourself out first, and why for a Stoic sorting yourself out begins and ends with your mind. The wise are not born but made. They make progress toward wisdom by cultivating a "large mind" (*magnus animus*) and achieving "large-mindedness"

or "magnanimity," the quality that ensures (among other things) that they always give others exactly what they deserve—in every way, from material goods to personal respect, and even punishment—and are therefore always fair. This Stoic sense of magnanimity—the goal we should all strive to achieve, however often we fail—is the subject of our first chapter.

A word on translation. I have tried both to be faithful to the Latin texts and to provide English versions that will strike contemporary readers as at least clear and idiomatic. But there is one point on which my translations slightly but consistently depart from the Latin. When Seneca refers to a wise person he writes either *vir sapiens* ("wise man"), with the strongly gendered noun *vir* ("adult male person"), or just the adjective, *sapiens*, used as a substantive—and no doubt

he and his readers took the adjective to be grammatically masculine, implicitly referring to a *vir*. I chose not to follow him in this regard, in part because of our contemporary sensibilities, but most of all because exclusive use of the masculine actually distorts a distinctive aspect of Stoicism: for alone among ancient philosophical sects, Stoicism held that all adult human persons have the potential to achieve wisdom thanks to the way they are built by nature. "Wise person" or the alternating use of "wise man" and "wise woman" might therefore be an acceptable choice, though I think either one would begin to sound a bit artificial with repeated use. I therefore have consistently written "the wise," the plural idiom common in English when a definite article (which Latin lacks) combines with an adjective to denote a category of persons.[4]

HOW TO DO THE RIGHT THING

I

STRIVING FOR MAGNANIMITY

Felix qui ad meliora hunc impetum dedit:
ponet se extra ius dicionemque fortunae;
secunda temperabit, adversa comminuet.
(*Epistle* 39.3)

Animi magnitudine, qui numquam maior
est quam ubi aliena seposuit et fecit sibi
pacem nihil timendo, fecit sibi divitias nihil
concupiscendo. (*Epistle* 87.3)

I

STRIVING FOR MAGNANIMITY

Happy are those who strive to reach the good: they will have a place beyond fortune's jurisdiction, greeting success with moderation, reducing adversity to insignificance. (*Epistle* 39.3)

The largeness of a mind that is never greater than when it . . . has created peace for itself by fearing nothing, wealth by desiring nothing. (*Epistle* 87.3)

We can begin to understand the connection between fair dealing and being "large-minded"—and the reason why that trait is

the subject of this book's first chapter—by starting from a trait that is its very opposite. Most people reading this paragraph must have known at least one person they could describe as "small-minded." Such a person's view of the world is severely limited by their own experience and the lens of the self ("Well, if I could do X, I don't see why [some disfavored person or group] can't do it too"); by their own opinions, to which they cling stubbornly; and by their own goals, which tend to be narrow and self-interested. People like that—petty, fretful, inflexible, intolerant, often vehemently so—seem constitutionally incapable of adopting another person's point of view, or at least pausing to consider it calmly and clearly, and constitutionally incapable of being either critical of themselves or generous toward others. And yet, as we will

see, Seneca took clear and calm thinking, critical self-awareness, and generosity to be absolutely central to treating others fairly. That is where the opposite trait—"large-mindedness," or "magnanimity"—comes in, for it incorporates the ability to be and do all the things that right dealing and fairness require. That is why it is worth getting a clear view of what such "large-mindedness" entails.[1]

According to a standard definition, English "magnanimity" denotes "loftiness of spirit enabling one to bear trouble calmly, to disdain meanness and pettiness, and to display a noble generosity" (Merriam-Webster). That description certainly shares a family relationship with ancient conceptions of "large-mindedness," including that of the Stoics, who believed that the largest mind—the mind of God—pervaded every

nook and cranny of the universe, giving it its providential order, and that it was the proper aim of human beings to try to approximate the God with whom—alone of all creatures—they share the gift of reason.

With that aim in view, in fact, the Stoics granted "magnanimity" a special standing that the definition just quoted only begins to touch. Suppose that you had a mind so capacious and sharp that it always perceived every circumstance with complete accuracy, recognizing it for what it truly was, then evaluated it thoroughly and correctly, decided unerringly what if anything to do about it, planned perfectly whatever it was that needed doing, and provided all the resolve needed to do it. You would indeed have a "large mind," a perfectly virtuous mind—in fact, the mind of a wise person

that (as Seneca several times says) differs from the mind of God only in being mortal.[2] Such a mind would provide the grounding for all right behavior by providing a sound view of the world and establishing a sound set of priorities for action. Needless to say, such a mind would always prompt us to treat others fairly; also needless to say, it is a condition of mind that (at most) very, very few actual humans have achieved. So how can we best imagine what it would be like truly to achieve it?

Seneca uses several devices to answer that question and make the all-but-impossible graspable, for example by trying to sketch "the fine and holy sight we'd see" if we could look upon the mind of a wise and good person, or by conjuring up some of the very few historical persons who might seem to have achieved the ideal. In this way

the passages that follow set a higher bar for virtuous behavior than most of us can clear but also point toward the reachable goals that the subsequent chapters describe.

These first two passages, both from the *Moral Epistles*, stress qualities or principles that recur time and again in all of Seneca's writings: the need to ignore the vagaries of common opinion and look to the permanent truth of nature; the contented and self-contained tranquility that is the hallmark of virtue; the possibility of making progress toward virtue, and the freedom it brings, if you put in the necessary work; and the unity of virtue—the principle that if you are loyal, brave, and pious you are necessarily also generous, prudent, and fair—with "magnanimity looming above all."

(7) Dicam quomodo intellegas sanum: si se ipse contentus est, si confidit sibi, si scit omnia vota mortalium, omnia beneficia quae dantur petunturque, nullum in beata vita habere momentum. Nam cui aliquid accedere potest, id inperfectum est; cui aliquid abscedere potest, id inperpetuum est: cuius perpetua futura laetitia est, is suo gaudeat. . . . Sed haec quoque fortuita tunc delectant cum illa ratio temperavit ac miscuit: haec est quae etiam externa commendet, quorum avidis usus ingratus est. (8) Solebat Attalus hac imagine uti:

Vidisti aliquando canem missa a domino frusta panis aut carnis aperto ore captantem? quidquid recepit protinus integrum devorat et semper ad spem venturi hiat. Idem evenit nobis: quidquid expectantibus fortuna proiecit, id

(7) [You can] recognize a mind that is sound if it is content and confident, if it knows that all human desires, all favors granted and sought, have no bearing on the best human life. Whatever can be increased is imperfect, whatever can be lessened is impermanent: a mind that will know unending happiness should rejoice in its own resources. . . . Yet even fortune's gifts are pleasing when reason has blended and balanced them:[3] it is reason that makes them agreeable, while the greedy get no satisfaction from them. (8) Attalus[4] used to use this metaphor:

Have you ever seen a dog, jaws open wide, trying to snatch a bit of bread or meat its master has tossed? Whatever it gets, it immediately swallows whole and is always gaping hopefully for more. We're the same way: whatever

sine ulla voluptate demittimus statim,
ad rapinam alterius erecti et attoniti.
Hoc sapienti non evenit: plenus est;
etiam si quid obvenit, secure excipit ac
reponit; laetitia fruitur maxima, conti-
nua, sua. (*Epistle* 72.7–8)

(3) Si nobis animum boni viri liceret in-
spicere, o quam pulchram faciem, quam
sanctam, quam ex magnifico placidoque
fulgentem videremus, hinc iustitia, illinc
fortitudine, hinc temperantia prudenti-
aque lucentibus! Praeter has frugalitas et
continentia et tolerantia et liberalitas
bonum splendorem illi suum adfunde-
rent. Tunc providentia cum elegantia et
ex istis magnanimitas eminentissima

fortune tosses us as we wait we immediately swallow down without savor-
ing, frantically intent on snatching
more.
This does not happen to the wise: whatever comes along they calmly take up
and set aside, enjoying a happiness that
is very great, unending, all their own.
(*Epistle* 72.7–8)

(3) What a fine and holy sight we'd see if
we could observe the mind of a good person, its brilliance shining forth from a
place of tranquil splendor, with justice
and courage, moderation and prudence
gleaming on every side, and thrift, too,
and self-control, fortitude, and generosity
casting their fair light upon it. What glory,
what weight and dignity, what gracious
authority foresight and scrupulousness

quantum, di boni, decoris illi, quantum ponderis gravitatisque adderent! quanta esset cum gratia auctoritas! Nemo illam amabilem qui non simul venerabilem diceret. (4) Si quis viderit hanc faciem altiorem fulgentioremque quam cerni inter humana consuevit, nonne velut numinis occursu obstupefactus resistat et ut fas sit vidisse tacitus precetur, tum evocante ipsa vultus benignitate productus adoret ac supplicet. . . . (5) Aderit levabitque, si colere eam voluerimus. Colitur autem non taurorum opimis corporibus contrucidatis sed pia et recta voluntate. (6) Nemo, inquam, non amore eius arderet si nobis illam videre contingeret; nunc enim multa obstrigillant et aciem nostram aut splendore nimio repercutiunt aut obscuritate retinent. Sed si, quemadmodum visus oculorum quibusdam medicamentis acui

would add, and magnanimity looming above all. Every voice would declare the sight worthy of love and reverence. (4) Any who saw it, loftier and more brilliant than things human beings ordinarily see, would surely stop, stunned as at the appearance of a god, and silently pray that they had not transgressed in seeing it;[5] then led on by the inviting benevolence of its expression, they would bow in worship. . . . (5) [This god] will assist and raise us up, if we are devoted to it, with our devotion expressed not by the slaughtered bodies of choice bulls . . . but by a dutiful and upright will. (6) No one, as I said, would not burn with love, if it were our lot to see it. Now in fact there are many obstructions: our sight is either blinded by too much brilliance or frustrated by darkness. Yet as our

solet et repurgari, sic nos aciem animi liberare inpedimentis voluerimus, poterimus perspicere virtutem. (*Epistle* 115.3–6)

eyesight is often sharpened and made clear by certain medicines, if we willingly free our mind's vision from its impediments, we will be able to see virtue clearly. (*Epistle* 115.3–6)

Seneca knew—and frequently admitted—that he was not wise: he was just one of those trying to make progress toward wisdom, an attempt that was worth making even if the goal could not be reached. But there were a few—vanishingly few—who might be thought to have succeeded and so serve as exemplars for the rest of us. Socrates was probably the consensus choice: insisting that his fellow Athenians question their own beliefs and practices as searchingly as he questioned his own, he became a martyr to the cause of intellectual and moral independence. And for some Romans

(27) Si . . . exemplum desideratis, accipite Socraten, perpessicium senem, per omnia aspera iactatum, invictum tamen et paupertate . . . et laboribus, quos militares quoque pertulit. . . . †sivere† aut in bello fuit aut in tyrannide aut in libertate bellis ac tyrannis saeviore. (28) Viginti et septem annis pugnatum est; post finita arma

the younger Cato—a contemporary of Cicero and a professed Stoic—was another candidate:[6] after the rivalry of Julius Caesar and Pompey the Great led to the civil war that ended the Republic and set the stage for five centuries of autocratic rule, Cato came to be regarded as a man who rejected factionalism and cared only for freedom, choosing suicide when he could live only by accepting Caesar's clemency and the subservience he thought it implied.

(27) If you want a model, take Socrates, that long-suffering old man, buffeted by every sort of adversity, who was nonetheless unvanquished by poverty . . . and toil, including service endured under arms. . . . [He lived] either in war or under tyranny, or in a freedom crueler than wars and tyrants.[7] (28) The war lasted

triginta tyrannis noxae dedita est civitas, ex quibus plerique inimici erant. Novissime damnatio est sub gravissimis nominibus impleta: obiecta est et religionum violatio et iuventutis corruptela, quam inmittere in deos, in patres, in rem publicam dictus est. Post haec carcer et venenum. Haec usque eo animum Socratis non moverant ut ne vultum quidem moverint. <O> illam mirabilem laudem et singularem! usque ad extremum nec hilariorem quisquam nec tristiorem Socraten vidit; aequalis fuit in tanta inaequalitate fortunae.

(29) Vis alterum exemplum? accipe hunc M. Catonem recentiorem, cum quo et infestius fortuna egit et pertinacius. Cui cum omnibus locis obstitisset, novissime

twenty-seven years; after it ended, the state was surrendered like chattel to thirty tyrants, most of them Socrates's enemies. Finally, there is his condemnation on the most serious charges: he was accused of violating religious norms and corrupting the youth, whom he supposedly turned against the gods, their fathers, and the civil community. Prison and poison followed. All this was so far from moving Socrates's mind that it didn't even alter his expression. What wonderful and singular glory, that to the end no one saw Socrates especially elated or downcast: amid such vicissitudes of fortune he was unchanged.

(29) Do you want another model? Take Cato the younger, whom fortune more insistently treated with greater malice. Though fortune had stymied him

et in morte, ostendit tamen virum for-
tem posse invita fortuna vivere, invita
mori. . . . (30) Nemo mutatum Catonem
totiens mutata re publica vidit; eundem se
in omni statu praestitit, in praetura, in repulsa, in accusatione, in provincia, in
contione, in exercitu, in morte. Denique
in illa rei publicae trepidatione, cum illinc
Caesar esset decem legionibus pugnacis-
simis subnixus, totis exterarum gentium
praesidiis, hinc Cn. Pompeius, satis unus
adversus omnia, cum alii ad Caesarem in-
clinarent, alii ad Pompeium, solus Cato
fecit aliquas et rei publicae partes. . . . (33)
Vides posse homines laborem pati: per
medias Africae solitudines pedes duxit
exercitum. Vides posse tolerari sitim: in

everywhere—finally even in death—he still showed that the brave can spite fortune by living and by dying.[8] . . . (30) No matter how often the Republic changed, no one saw a change in Cato: he showed himself to be the same in every circumstance, in high office or defeat, as prosecutor or provincial commander, in the assembly, in the army, in death. Finally, amid the Republic's upheaval—with Caesar on one side, supported by ten legions eager for war and allied with all foreign nations, Pompey on the other side, one man ready to face all adversity—as some supported Caesar, others Pompey, Cato alone saw to it that the Republic, too, had a partisan. . . . (33) You see that human beings can endure travail: Cato, on foot, led his army through the midst of the African desert. You see that thirst

collibus arentibus sine ullis inpedimentis
victi exercitus reliquias trahens inopiam
umoris loricatus tulit et, quotiens aquae
fuerat occasio, novissimus bibit. Vides
honorem et notam posse contemni:
eodem quo repulsus est die in comitio
pila lusit. Vides posse non timeri potentiam superiorum: et Pompeium et Caesarem, quorum nemo alterum offendere
audebat nisi ut alterum demereretur,
simul provocavit. Vides tam mortem
posse contemni quam exilium: et exilium
sibi indixit et mortem et interim bellum.
(34) Possumus itaque adversus ista tantum habere animi, libeat modo subdu-
cere iugo collum. . . . Aurum et argentum
et quidquid aliud felices domos onerat

can be endured: dragging the remnant of his army, vanquished and without supplies, along the parched hills, he went without water in heavy armor, and, when the chance to drink arose, he drank last. You see that office and distinction can be despised: he played a game of ball on the very day he lost his election.[9] You see that one need not fear those with greater power: though all others dared to offend the one only if doing so secured the other's favor, Cato challenged Pompey and Caesar together. You see that death can be despised as easily as exile: he imposed on himself both exile and death, and in between them war.[10] (34) So we can face such adversities with just as much spirit, once we shake the yoke from our necks. . . . Leave behind gold and silver and whatever else burdens prosperous

relinquatur: non potest gratis constare libertas. Hanc si magno aestimas, omnia parvo aestimanda sunt. (*Epistle* 104.27–30, 33–34)

(7) Ad [Idomenea] Epicurus illam nobilem sententiam scripsit qua hortatur ut Pythoclea locupletem non publica nec ancipiti via faciat. "Si vis" inquit "Pythoclea divitem facere, non pecuniae

households: freedom cannot be had for nothing. If you value freedom highly, all else must be thought cheap. (*Epistle* 104.27–30, 33–34)

Now, few of us can hope to become paragons of wisdom, but figures such as Socrates and Cato point to a goal that is actually within reach: developing a good will—a will that aims only at the good—which can be achieved, as Seneca urges in these next passages, if we diminish our desires, understand that a "good mind" is available to all people, and work every day to achieve it.

(7) Epicurus wrote this noble thought to Idomeneus, urging him to make Pythocles rich in no common or ambiguous way:[11] "If you want to make Pythocles wealthy, don't increase his funds, lessen

adiciendum sed cupiditati detrahendum est." (8) Et apertior ista sententia est quam <ut> interpretanda sit, et disertior quam ut adiuvanda. Hoc unum te admoneo, ne istud tantum existimes de divitîs dictum: quocumque transtuleris, idem poterit. Si vis Pythoclea honestum facere, non honoribus adiciendum est sed cupiditatibus detrahendum; si vis Pythoclea esse in perpetua voluptate, non voluptatibus adiciendum est sed cupiditatibus detrahendum; si vis Pythoclea senem facere et implere vitam, non annis adiciendum est sed cupiditatibus detrahendum. (*Epistle* 21.7–8)

(1) Iterum tu mihi te pusillum facis et dicis malignius tecum egisse naturam prius, deinde fortunam, cum possis eximere te vulgo et ad felicitatem hominum

his desires." (8) The point is too clear to need interpreting and too neat to need embellishing. One thing I do urge: don't suppose that the saying applies only to wealth. Change the frame of reference; its force stays the same. If you want to make Pythocles honorable, don't increase his honors, lessen his desires. If you want Pythocles to enjoy unending pleasure, don't increase his pleasures, lessen his desires. If you want Pythocles to reach old age living a full life, don't add to his years, lessen his desires. (*Epistle* 21.7–8)

(1) Again you belittle yourself, saying that first nature short-changed you, then fortune, though you're poised to escape from the common run of men and reach the pinnacle of human happiness [that is, wisdom]. If philosophy is good for

maximam emergere. Si quid est aliud in philosophia boni, hoc est, quod stemma non inspicit; omnes, si ad originem primam revocantur, a dis sunt. (2) Eques Romanus es, et ad hunc ordinem tua te perduxit industria; at mehercules multis quattuordecim clausa sunt, non omnes curia admittit, castra quoque quos ad laborem et periculum recipiant fastidiose legunt: bona mens omnibus patet, omnes ad hoc sumus nobiles. Nec reicit quemquam philosophia nec eligit: omnibus lucet. (*Epistle* 44.1–2)

(5) Nemo difficulter ad naturam reducitur nisi qui ab illa defecit: erubescimus discere bonam mentem. At mehercules, <si> turpe est magistrum huius rei quaerere, illud desperandum est, posse nobis casu tantum bonum influere: laborandum

anything, it is this: it doesn't look to pedigree; everyone—traced back to their beginnings—comes from the gods. (2) You're a Roman knight, and you've raised yourself to that rank through your own effort.[12] But good grief, the first fourteen rows are closed to many; the Senate house doesn't let everyone in; the army camp is choosy about whom it admits to its toil and danger: a good mind is available to all. We're all nobles in that regard. Philosophy neither rejects nor selects: it shines for all. (*Epistle* 44.1–2)

(5) Only those who have left nature's way have a hard time being led back: learning to have a good mind embarrasses us. But for heaven's sake, if shame forbids us to seek a teacher for this purpose, there is no hope at all that so great a good can just

est et, ut verum dicam, ne labor quidem magnus est, si modo . . . ante animum nostrum formare incipimus et recorrigere quam indurescat pravitas eius. . . . (7) . . . Non est quod te inpediat quominus de nobis bene speres, quod malitia nos iam tenet, quod diu in possessione nostri est: ad neminem ante bona mens venit quam mala; omnes praeoccupati sumus; virtutes discere vitia dediscere <est>. (8) Sed eo maiore animo ad emendationem nostri debemus accedere quod semel traditi nobis boni perpetua possessio est; non dediscitur virtus. (*Epistle* 50.5, 7–8)

chance to sink in by itself. It takes work and—to tell the truth—the work entailed is not even considerable, if only . . . we begin to shape and straighten our own mind before wrongheadedness becomes immoveable. . . . (7) . . . There is no reason not to have hope just because vice holds us firmly and has done so for a long time: one comes to have a good mind only after having a bad one. Because vice came to us first, unlearning it is the way to learn virtue. (8) But we should approach our self-correction all the more optimistically because once good has been passed on to us, possession of it is secure forever: there is no unlearning virtue. (*Epistle* 50.5, 7–8)

And to reach the goal of a good will in a large mind, we must cultivate two other goods that are the source of every virtue:

(32) Cito hoc potest tradi et paucissimis verbis: unum bonum esse virtutem, nullum certe sine virtute, et ipsam virtutem in parte nostri meliore, id est rationali, positam. Quid erit haec virtus? iudicium verum et inmotum; ab hoc enim impetus venient mentis, ab hoc omnis species quae impetum movet redigetur ad liquidum. . . . (36) Instemus itaque et perseveremus; plus quam profligavimus restat, sed magna pars est profectus velle proficere. Huius rei conscius mihi sum: volo et mente tota volo. Te quoque instinctum esse et magno ad pulcherrima properare impetu video. Properemus. (*Epistle* 71.32, 36)

clear thinking and true judgment, the sub-jects of the next chapter.

(32) This lesson can be taught quickly, in very few words: the only good is virtue, there certainly is no good without virtue, and virtue itself is placed in the better—that is, rational—part of us. What will this virtue be? True and unshakeable judg-ment: this will be the source of the mind's impulses; this will clarify every impres-sion that stirs an impulse. . . . (36) So let's press on and persevere: what remains is greater than what we've overcome, but a great part of progress is the willingness to progress. I know of myself that this is true: I am willing, and willing with all my mind. I see that you too have been roused and press on energetically toward this fairest goal. Let's hurry. (*Epistle* 71.32, 36)

2

BEING CALM, THINKING CLEARLY

Sola sublimis et excelsa virtus est, nec
quicquam magnum est nisi quod simul
placidum. (*On Anger* 1.21.4)

2

BEING CALM, THINKING CLEARLY

> Only virtue is lofty and exalted, nor is
> anything great if it is not also calm.
> (*On Anger* 1.21.4)

The wise always do right by others, the Stoics held, just as they always act bravely and speak truthfully, simply because, being wise, they can act and speak in no other way. The rest of us—the nonwise—must expend some effort to cultivate the clarity of mind that is the essential precondition of all virtues, fairness included.

To understand the importance that Seneca and the Stoics placed on clear thinking, consider their take on one of our ordinary human emotions—say, fear. On their understanding (which I happen to accept) my experiencing one run-of-the-mill sort of fear—the fear of physical harm—is based on my accepting as true two impressions or beliefs: that physical harm is a bad thing for me, and that a source of physical harm—for example, a massive, vicious dog intent on tearing out my throat—is present or approaching. If I accept that each of these premises is true, I will experience all the familiar physical and mental manifestations of fear: a "sinking" feeling in my stomach, an increased rate of breathing, a panicky agitation that unsettles my thoughts, a trembling or paralysis in my limbs, and so on. And on the Stoic view, I will be absolutely

mistaken to experience any of that, because—to set aside the massive dog for a moment—I will be absolutely mistaken to accept as true the belief that physical harm is a bad thing for me.

As we saw in the introduction, the predicate "is a bad thing for me" can be true if and only if its subject is "the absence of virtue"—the moral and intellectual failure caused by the mind's falling away from reason. The belief that physical harm is a bad thing for me is no more true and acceptable than the belief that physical well-being is a good thing for me, because harm and well-being are neither good nor bad things. They are "indifferents," and while we would be correct to prefer well-being over harm and to seek the one while we avoid the other, we would be wrong to think that our true human good would be at stake in

the seeking or in the avoiding. And so—to get back to the massive, vicious dog—the truly wise, confronted with the impression that the dog is about to attack, will experience "caution," the "good" emotion that corresponds to the nonwise person's "fear." They will be calm, not agitated; their thinking will be clear, not panicky. As a result, they might see that the dog is not as large as the first impression suggested and is not vicious but high-spirited; or if the dog really does intend them harm, they will have the presence of mind that can allow them to distract the dog, or soothe it, or avoid the attack in some other way. And if in the end the dog does pounce—well, that really is no bad thing: the wise will be joyful with the dog at their throat, just as they would be on a torturer's rack, because their minds will be at one with the reason that

governs the universe, and they will recognize that the dog is just a four-legged manifestation of divine providence.

And yes, I agree, "magnanimity" of that sort of is a lot to expect us to manage; and, again, Seneca does not really expect us to manage it. But he does encourage us to try — to practice the clear thinking, for example, that will allow us to see that an apparent insult was no such thing, or to reject the impression that an insult does us real harm. And so he has a good deal to say about the habits of mind that will help us to make progress toward wisdom, starting with the first step: be calm; avoid the restlessness that besets us when (as Seneca puts it) we "exert ourselves over trivialities." Above all, because the influence of other people's opinions is the primary reason why we fail to live "according to nature," we

(6) Omnes in eadem causa sunt, et hi qui levitate uexantur ac taedio adsiduaque mutatione propositi, quibus semper magis placet quod reliquerunt, et illi qui marcent et oscitantur. Adice eos qui non aliter quam quibus difficilis somnus est versant se et hoc atque illo modo componunt donec quietem lassitudine

should question those opinions and think for ourselves. If we do, we will be one step closer to thinking with a good will, intending to do what is right and attempting to put that intention into effect.

Of course, keeping calm is easier said than done, as Seneca well knew: here is a partial catalogue of the psychic woes that block our path and slow our progress, presented near the start of his treatise on tranquility.

(6) Everyone is in the same fix, both the feckless, troubled souls who constantly change their goals out of boredom, only to find that they prefer what they abandoned, and the apathetic types who yawn their lives away. Then there are those who toss and turn like insomniacs, arranging themselves this way and that until

inveniant: statum vitae suae reformando subinde in eo novissime manent in quo illos non mutandi odium sed senectus ad novandum pigra deprendit. . . . (7) Innumerabiles deinceps proprietates sunt sed unus effectus vitii, sibi displicere. Hoc oritur ab intemperie animi et cupiditatibus timidis aut parum prosperis, ubi aut non audent quantum concupiscunt aut non consequuntur et in spem toti prominent; semper instabiles mobilesque sunt, quod necesse est accidere pendentibus. . . . (8) Tunc illos et paenitentia coepti tenet et incipiendi timor subrepitque illa animi iactatio non invenientis exitum, quia nec imperare cupiditatibus suis nec obsequi possunt. . . . (10) Hinc illud est taedium et displicentia sui et nusquam residentis

exhaustion brings them rest: repeatedly refashioning their way of life, they're finally overtaken, not by distaste for change, but by a senile lack of energy for change. . . . (7) This vice has innumerable traits but just one result: self-loathing. It arises from a mind not well balanced and from longings either too cautious or too unprofitable, when people's desire exceeds their daring or failure leaves them grasping only at hope. They're never steady and still—inevitably, since they're always up in the air. . . . (8) Then regret for what they've undertaken grips them and fear of making a start; the agitation of a mind that sees no way out comes over them, incapable of either commanding or obeying their desires. . . . (10) Hence that boredom and self-loathing, the spinning of a mind that is never at rest and the

animi volutatio et otii sui tristis atque aegra patientia, utique ubi causas fateri pudet et tormenta introsus egit verecundia, in angusto inclusae cupiditates sine exitu se ipsae strangulant; inde maeror marcorque et mille fluctus mentis incertae, quam spes inchoatae suspensam habent, deploratae tristem. . . . (11) ex hac deinde aversatione alienorum processuum et suorum desperatione obirascens fortunae animus et de saeculo querens et in angulos se retrahens et poenae incubans suae, dum illum taedet sui pigetque. (*On Tranquility of Mind* 2.6–8, 10–11)

morose and queasy sufferance of unfilled time—how could it be otherwise, when acknowledging the cause prompts a blush and the torment is suppressed out of shame, when unvented desires are strangled by their close confinement. Grief and wasting result; the mind, unresolved, heaves on a thousand waves, anxious over hopes only sketched, depressed at hopes abandoned. . . . (11) Repelled by others' successes, despairing of its own, the mind grows furious with fortune, laments the times, withdraws into its recesses, and sulks at being punished, fed up and disgusted with itself. (*On Tranquility of Mind* 2.6–8, 10–11)

The feckless and the apathetic, the frantic and the regretful, the hopeful and the despairing—they all share one trait: a lack of

(2) Harpasten, uxoris meae fatuam, scis hereditarium onus in domo mea remansisse. Ipse enim aversissimus ab istis prodigiis sum; si quando fatuo delectari volo, non est mihi longe quaerendus: me rideo. Haec fatua subito desiit videre. Incredibilem rem tibi narro, sed veram: nescit esse se caecam; subinde

self-knowledge. Even when they are aware that all is not well, they do not know why: whereas the wise know that they are wise, and live contented, the nonwise do not know that they are fools and so do not know the cause of their malaise. Seneca illustrates the point with an anecdote about one of the enslaved members of his household, who served his wife as a kind of jester:

(2) You know that Harpastê, my wife's fool, remains in our household as an inherited burden.[1] I myself want nothing at all to do with such creatures: if I ever want to be amused by a fool, I don't have far to look — I laugh at myself. After suddenly becoming blind — the story is unbelievable but true — this fool doesn't realize that she is blind but repeatedly

paedagogum suum rogat ut migret, ait domum tenebricosam esse. (3) Hoc quod in illa ridemus omnibus nobis accidere liqueat tibi: nemo se avarum esse intellegit, nemo cupidum. Caeci tamen ducem quaerunt, nos sine duce erramus et dicimus, "non ego ambitiosus sum, sed nemo aliter Romae potest vivere"; "non ego sumptuosus sum, sed urbs ipsa magnas inpensas exigit"; "non est meum vitium quod iracundus sum, quod nondum constitui certum genus vitae: adulescentia haec facit." (4) Quid nos decipimus? non est extrinsecus malum nostrum: intra nos est, in visceribus ipsis sedet, et ideo difficulter ad sanitatem pervenimus quia nos aegrotare nescimus. Si curari coeperimus, quando tot morborum tantas vires discutiemus? Nunc vero ne quaerimus

asks her attendant to move her, saying her apartment is too dark. (3) It should be clear to you that what makes us laugh in her case happens to us all: no one sees that he is greedy or grasping. Yet the blind need a guide while we wander unattended and say, "I am not ambitious—but it's impossible to live otherwise in Rome"; "I am not a spendthrift—but the city demands large outlays"; "I am inclined to anger—but it's not my fault, I haven't yet settled on a stable sort of life, my youth's the cause." (4) Why do we deceive ourselves? The cause of distress lies not outside us but within; it is settled in our very vitals, and because we do not know that we are ailing it is hard to find relief. If we do start on a cure, when will we shake off the diseases—they are legion, and very powerful? Yet now we do not even seek

quidem medicum, qui minus negotii ha-
beret si adhiberetur ad recens vitium;
sequerentur teneri et rudes animi recta
monstrantem. (*Epistle* 50.2–4)

12 (1) Proximum ab his erit ne aut in su-
pervacuis aut ex supervacuo laboremus,
id est ne quae aut non possumus consequi concupiscamus aut adepti vanitatem
cupiditatium nostrarum sero post multum sudorem intellegamus, id est ne aut
labor inritus sit sine effectu aut effectus

a physician, who would have an easier time if summoned to address a fresh fault: our minds, pliant and unformed, would follow directions to the right path. (*Epistle* 50.2–4)

The road to tranquility begins with reflection: consider where your energy should be directed, and why; pare away everything irrelevant to the peace of mind that is your proper goal; and be prepared for the stroke of bad luck that frustrates your aim.

12 (1) Next, we should not exert ourselves over trivialities or from trivial motives: let's not desire what we cannot achieve or—having achieved it—recognize too late, after much sweat, that our desires were empty. Let our efforts not fail to produce results, let the results not be

labore indignus; fere enim ex his tristitia sequitur, si aut non successit aut successus pudet. (2) Circumcidenda concursatio, qualis est magnae parti hominum domos et theatra et fora pererrantium: alienis se negotiis offerunt, semper aliquid agentibus similes. Horum si aliquem exeuntem e domo interrogaveris "quo tu? quid cogitas?" respondebit tibi "non mehercules scio; sed aliquos videbo, aliquid agam." (3) Sine proposito vagantur quaerentes negotia nec quae destinaverunt agunt sed in quae incurrerunt: inconsultus illis vanusque cursus est. . . . His plerique similem vitam agunt, quorum non inmerito quis inquietam inertiam dixerit. (4) Quorundam quasi ad incendium currentium misereberis: usque eo

unworthy of our efforts, for despondency follows both from failure and from success that brings disgrace. (2) We should be less inclined to dash about, this way and that, as most people do, wandering from house to house, theater to theater, forum to forum, volunteering to further others' interests, like movers and shakers. If you ask one of them as he is leaving home, "Where to, what's the plan?," he will reply, "God, I have no idea, but I'll see some people, make something happen." (3) They wander randomly, looking for occupation, and do what comes their way, not what they had in mind: they are just on the run, thoughtlessly and aimlessly. . . . Most people live that way — fidgety indolence, one could call it. (4) Pitiable, some of them are, like people rushing to a fire, thrusting aside those

inpellunt obvios et se aliosque praecipi-
tant, cum interim cucurrerunt aut saluta-
turi aliquem non resalutaturum aut funus
ignoti hominis prosecuturi. ... Dein
domum cum supervacua redeuntes lassitudine iurant nescire se ipsos quare exie-
rint, ubi fuerint, postero die erraturi per
eadem illa vestigia. (5) Omnis itaque labor
aliquo referatur, aliquo respiciat. Non industria inquietos sed insanos falsae
rerum imagines agitant ... : proritat illos
alicuius rei species, cuius vanitatem capta
mens non coarguit.

13 (2) Nam qui multa agit saepe fortunae
potestatem sui facit, quam tutissimum est
raro experiri, ceterum semper de illa cogitare et nihil sibi de fide eius promittere:
"navigabo, nisi si quid inciderit" ... et

they meet, sending themselves and others headlong—meanwhile, they have run to attend some stranger's funeral or to call on someone who will not return their greeting. . . . Arriving back home, exhausted and with nothing to show for their effort, they swear they themselves do not know why they left, where they went—destined to wander over the same track tomorrow. (5) So let all our effort be directed at some goal. Diligence does not make people restless, but phantoms drive them crazy: some impression goads them on, and their enslaved minds do not see it for the empty thing it is.

13 (2) Someone active on many fronts often submits to fortune, which is safest when rarely tested but kept always in mind and never reckoned reliable: "I will sail—absent some chance occurrence" . . .

"negotiatio mihi respondebit, nisi si quid intervenerit." (3) Hoc est quare sapienti nihil contra opinionem dicamus accidere: non illum casibus hominum excerpimus sed erroribus nec illi omnia ut voluit cedunt, sed ut cogitavit; in primis autem cogitavit aliquid posse propositis suis resistere. Necesse est autem levius ad animum pervenire destitutae cupiditatis dolorem cui successum non utique promiseris. (*On Tranquility of Mind* 12.1–5, 13.2–3)

and "The deal will go my way—absent some obstacle." (3) This is why we say that nothing unexpected happens to the wise: we exempt them from humanity's common errors, not its misfortunes, and everything turns out, not as they wished, but as they expected—having expected above all that something could oppose their plans. Inevitably, the pain of disappointed desire more lightly touches a mind to which you haven't promised success. (*On Tranquility of Mind* 12.1–5, 13.2–3)

Above all—a point Seneca repeatedly makes—we should remember that thanks to the way we were built by nature, we have from birth all that we need for a good life and true happiness. We should resist the influence of opinions around us that make us

(6) Quam multa autem paramus quia alii paraverunt! ... Inter causas malorum nostrorum est quod vivimus ad exempla, nec ratione componimur sed consuetudine abducimur. Quod si pauci facerent nollemus imitari, cum plures facere coeperunt, quasi honestius sit quia frequentius, sequimur; et recti apud nos locum tenet error ubi publicus factus est. (7) Omnes iam sic peregrinantur ut illos Numidarum praecurrat equitatus, ut agmen cursorum antecedat: turpe est nullos esse qui occurrentis via deiciant, [ut] qui honestum hominem venire

edgy and unsettled by promoting false goals and specious goods.

(6) We acquire so many things because others have acquired them! . . . The fact that we model our lives on others' is one source of our problems: we do not organize our lives according to reason but are led astray by fashion. Behavior we would not willingly imitate if we saw it only in a few we adopt when we see more people behaving that way, as if greater currency made it more honorable: once wrong becomes common it supplants right in our minds. (7) So now everyone travels with Numidian horsemen riding before them and a column of runners in the vanguard: it's a disgrace not to have attendants to sweep from the path those they meet and raise a dust cloud to mark a bigshot's

magno pulvere ostendant. Omnes iam mulos habent qui crustallina et murrina et caelata magnorum artificum manu portent: turpe est videri eas te habere sarcinas solas quae tuto concuti possint. . . .

(8) Horum omnium sermo vitandus est: hi sunt qui vitia tradunt et alio aliunde transferunt. . . . Horum sermo multum nocet; nam etiam si non statim proficit, semina in animo relinquit sequiturque nos etiam cum ab illis discessimus, resurrecturum postea malum. (9) Quemadmodum qui audierunt synphoniam ferunt secum in auribus modulationem illam ac dulcedinem cantuum, quae cogitationes inpedit nec ad seria patitur intendi, sic adulatorum et prava laudantium sermo diutius haeret quam auditur. Nec facile est animo dulcem sonum excutere: prosequitur et

approach. Now everyone has mules to carry cups of crystal and agate, embossed in gold by great craftsmen: it's a shame to be seen to have only such baggage as can safely take a beating. . . .

(8) Do not converse with all these people: they are the ones who transmit faults, passing them along from one to another. . . . Their talk does a lot of harm, for even if it does not have immediate effect, it plants seeds in the mind and pursues us when we have left their company, an evil that will reassert itself later. (9) As a concert's audience carries away in its ears the melody and sweet song, impeding reflection and keeping thought from taking a serious turn, so the corrupt chatter of flatterers and sycophants lingers after it's heard. It is hard to banish the pleasing sound from one's mind:

durat et ex intervallo recurrit. Ideo clu-
dendae sunt aures malis vocibus et quidem
primis. (*Epistle* 123.6–9)

(2) Ad summam sapiens eris, si cluseris
aures, quibus ceram parum est obdere:
firmiore spissamento opus est quam in
sociis usum Ulixem ferunt. Illa vox quae
timebatur erat blanda, non tamen publica: at haec quae timenda est non ex
uno scopulo sed ex omni terrarum parte
circumsonat. . . . Surdum te amantissimis
tuis praesta: bono animo mala precantur.
Et si esse vis felix, deos ora ne quid tibi
ex his quae optantur eveniat. (3) Non
sunt ista bona quae in te isti volunt con-
geri: unum bonum est, quod beatae vitae

it follows along, it abides, it returns later on. We must therefore shut our ears to mischievous voices, right from the start. (*Epistle* 123.6–9)

(2) In short, you will be wise to shut your ears, a job for which wax is not enough: you need a sturdier plug than they say Odysseus used on his companions.[2] The voice they feared was alluring, yet not all-pervasive: the voice you should fear resounds not from a single crag but from every corner of the earth. . . . Turn a deaf ear to your nearest and dearest: with every good intention they pray for things that would harm you. If you want to be happy, beg the gods to frustrate all their wishes. (3) The things they would have heaped upon you are not good: there is only one good, the cause and guarantee

causa et firmamentum est, sibi fidere. (*Epistle* 31.2–3)

1 (3) Nihil ergo magis praestandum est quam ne pecorum ritu sequamur antecedentium gregem, pergentes non quo eundum est sed quo itur. Atqui nulla res nos maioribus malis inplicat quam quod ad rumorem componimur . . . quodque exempla <nobis pro> bonis multa sunt nec ad rationem sed ad similitudinem vivimus. (4) . . . Quod in strage hominum magna evenit, cum ipse se populus premit—nemo ita cadit ut non et alium in se adtrahat, primique exitio sequentibus sunt—hoc in omni vita accidere videas licet. Nemo sibi tantummodo errat, sed alieni erroris et causa et auctor est. . . .

of the best human life—self-reliance. (*Epistle* 31.2–3)

1 (3) The most important thing is this: that we not, like cattle, just follow the herd ahead of us, going where it happens to go, not where we should go. And yet nothing gets us into more trouble than organizing our lives according to what people say; . . . having many models, not good ones; and living not according to reason but by mimicry. (4) . . . When people press against each other in a great tumult, no one falls without dragging another on top of him, the foremost bringing destruction upon those behind—you can see this happen in all our lives. No one's errors touch him alone, but they are the cause and warrant of another's.

2 (2) Quaeramus ergo quid optimum factu sit, non quid usitatissimum, et quid nos in possessione felicitatis aeternae constituat, non quid vulgo, veritatis pessimo interpreti, probatum sit. . . . Habeo melius et certius lumen quo a falsis vera diiudicem: animi bonum animus inveniat. Hic, si umquam respirare illi et recedere in se vacaverit, o quam sibi ipse verum tortus a se fatebitur ac dicet: (3) "Quidquid feci adhuc infectum esse mallem, quidquid dixi cum recogito, mutis invideo. . . . Omnem operam dedi ut me multitudini educerem et aliqua dote notabilem facerem: quid aliud quam . . . me . . . malevolentiae quod morderet ostendi? (4) . . . Quin potius quaero aliquod usu bonum, quod sentiam, non quod

2 (2) Let's ask, then, what it is best to do, not what is most commonly done, and what will make us happy forever, not what is approved by the general public, the truth's worst interpreter. . . . I have a better, more reliable light to use in distinguishing the true from the false: let the mind discover the mind's own good. If ever the mind is free to catch its breath and rely on its own resources, how it will rack itself and confess the truth, saying, (3) "Whatever I have done, I would wish it was yet undone; when I recall all that I have said, I envy the mute. . . . I have made every effort to distinguish myself from the many and make myself noteworthy through some talent: what have I achieved beyond exposing myself to a gnawing malice? (4) . . . Why not rather seek some good that I can actually experience, not

ostendam? Ista quae spectantur, ad quae consistitur, quae alter alteri stupens monstrat, foris nitent, introrsus misera sunt." (*On the Happy Life* 1.3–4, 2.2–4)

(1) Quidni tu, mi Lucili, maximum putes instrumentum vitae beatae hanc persuasionem unum bonum esse quod honestum est? Nam qui alia bona iudicat in fortunae venit potestatem, alieni arbitrii fit:

hold out for show? The things that catch the eye and draw a crowd, that one astonished person points out to another—they are glittering on the outside but are wretched within." (*On the Happy Life* 1.3–4, 2.2–4)

If we think for ourselves, using the reason that nature gave us instead of aping the preferences of others, we can more reliably think clearly, more quickly come to see that virtue is the only worthy goal, and more surely direct our intentions toward it:

(1) My dear Lucilius, why shouldn't you think that the best means to secure the best human life is the conviction that what is honorable is the only good? For one who judges other things good falls under fortune's power, subject to

qui omne bonum honesto circumscripsit intra se felix <est>. (2) Hic amissis liberis maestus, hic sollicitus aegris, hic turpibus et aliqua sparsis infamia tristis; illum videbis alienae uxoris amore cruciari, illum suae; non deerit quem repulsa distorqueat; erunt quos ipse honor vexet. . . . (4) Occurrent acti in exilium et evoluti bonis; . . . occurrent naufragi similiave naufragis passi, quos aut popularis ira aut invidia . . . inopinantis securosque disiecit procellae more . . . aut fulminis subiti ad cuius ictum etiam vicina tremuerunt. Nam ut illic quisquis ab igne

another's judgment: the one for whom the good is indistinguishable from the honorable has happiness within himself. (2) This person is grief stricken when his children die, or troubled when they are ill, or downcast if they are disgraced and stained by ill repute; that person you will see tormented by love for another's wife, yet another by love for his own; you will find some racked by electoral loss, others troubled by the very office they won. . . . (4) You will come upon men driven into exile, stripped of their wealth, . . . others who have suffered shipwreck, or something like it, whom the people's anger or envy unexpectedly struck down when they were carefree, like a sudden squall . . . or a lightning bolt at whose blast even the neighboring regions tremble. For as in

propior stetit percusso similis obstipuit,
sic in his per aliquam vim accidentibus
unum calamitas opprimit, ceteros metus,
paremque passis tristitiam facit pati
posse. . . . (6) Quisquis se multum fortu-
itis dedit ingentem sibi materiam pertur-
bationis et inexplicabilem fecit: una haec
via est ad tuta vadenti, externa despicere
et honesto esse contentum. Nam qui aliquid virtute melius putat aut ullum praeter illam bonum, ad haec quae a fortuna
sparguntur sinum expandit et sollicitus
missilia eius expectat.

(7) Hanc enim imaginem animo tuo
propone, ludos facere Fortunam et in
hunc mortalium coetum honores, divitias, gratiam excutere, quorum alia inter

the latter case whoever stands too close to the blast is as stunned as the one who was struck, so in these other chance upheavals disaster overwhelms one person, fear all others: the potential for suffering makes them as distressed as those who have actually suffered. . . . (6) Whoever surrenders to chance gives anxiety much raw material to work with, making it inescapable: disdaining external things, being content with what is honorable, is the one path to safety. For those who reckon that there is some good preferable to or other than virtue bare their breasts to whatever fortune throws at them: they uneasily await its darts.

(7) Set this image before your mind. Fortune is holding games and scatters offices, riches, influence among the gathered mortals: some of these gifts are torn

diripientium manus scissa sunt, alia infida societate divisa, alia magno detrimento eorum in quos devenerant prensa. Ex quibus quaedam aliud agentibus inciderunt, quaedam, quia nimis captabantur, amissa . . . sunt: nulli vero, etiam cui rapina feliciter cessit, gaudium rapti duravit in posterum. Itaque prudentissimus quisque, cum primum induci videt munuscula, a theatro fugit et scit magno parva constare. . . . (8) Idem in his evenit quae fortuna desuper iactat: aestuamus miseri, distringimur, multas habere cupimus manus, modo in hanc partem, modo in illam respicimus. . . . (9) . . . Gaudemus si quid invasimus invadendique aliquos spes vana delusit. . . . Secedamus itaque ab

to bits by the hands that clutch them, others are divvied up in unreliable partnerships, others seized to the detriment of those who caught them. Some land on people whose attention is directed elsewhere, others are lost by being snatched too eagerly: no one—not even the one who comes away with some loot—finds a lasting joy in what they have grabbed. So all the shrewdest people leave the theater as soon as the gifts are spied, knowing that those trifles come at a heavy cost. . . . (8) The same thing happens with the things that fortune rains upon us: in a lather, wretched, we are pulled in different directions, wishing we had more than two hands as we look now this way, now that. . . . (9) . . . We rejoice when we seize something and when others' hopes of doing so are mocked. . . . So let's

istis ludis et demus raptoribus locum; illi spectent bona ista pendentia et ipsi magis pendeant. (10) Quicumque beatus esse constituet, unum esse bonum putet, quod honestum est. (*Epistle* 74.1–2, 4, 6–10)

withdraw from those games, yielding our places to the eager snatchers: let them look to the prizes dangled above them, and let them be in still more suspense themselves. (10) Whoever is resolved to live the best sort of life should reckon that what is honorable is the only good. (*Epistle* 74.1–2, 4, 6–10)

To illustrate the singular importance of forming a good intention the Stoics often used the example of an archer, whose skill consists of knowing how to seat the arrow properly, draw the bowstring to the right degree of tension, and release it smoothly and accurately toward the target. If the archer does all these things properly, he has done everything that was needed to demonstrate his skill, and he deserves to be considered a good archer: if after he releases the

(33) Ego . . . iudico nec artem gubernatoris deteriorem ulla tempestate fieri nec
ipsam administrationem artis. Guberna-
tor tibi non felicitatem promisit sed

bowstring a sudden gust of wind chances to blow the arrow off course, that has no bearing whatever on his skill and should have no bearing on our judgment of him. And as with archers, so with us. Having done what was in our power to do, we can be content with the outcome, whatever it happens to be: because they proceed from our own will, the intention and the attempt are the only things that we can truly and wholly call our own. Seneca makes much the same point using the example of a skilled helmsman in a storm:

(33) I judge . . . that no storm diminishes either the helmsman's skill or that skill's exercise. The helmsman promised you not a successful voyage but the effort that

utilem operam et navis regendae scien-
tiam; haec eo magis apparet quo illi magis
aliqua fortuita vis obstitit. Qui hoc potuit
dicere, "Neptune, numquam hanc navem
nisi rectam," arti satis fecit: tempestas non
opus gubernatoris inpedit sed successum.
(34) "Quid ergo?" inquit "non nocet gubernatori ea res quae illum tenere portum
vetat, quae conatus eius inritos efficit,
quae aut refert illum aut detinet et exar-
mat?" Non tamquam gubernatori, sed
tamquam naviganti nocet. . . . Gubernatoris artem adeo non inpedit ut ostendat;
tranquillo enim, ut aiunt, quilibet guber-
nator est. Navigio ista obsunt, non rectori
eius, qua rector est. (*Epistle* 85.33–34)

would be useful toward that end and his knowledge of steering a ship, which is made more manifest to the degree that random violence presents a greater challenge. The one who can say, "Neptune, never this ship save upright" has done what his expertise demands:[3] the storm hinders a successful outcome, not the helmsman's activity as helmsman. (34) "What then?," someone says, "is not the helmsman harmed by the thing that forbids him from making port?" It harms him, not in his capacity as helmsman, only as one making a voyage. . . . In fact so far from hindering the helmsman's skill, it puts it on display: for as they say, everyone is a helmsman on a flat sea. The circumstances you describe impede the ship, not the helmsman in his capacity as a helmsman. (*Epistle* 85.33–34)

In the next two chapters we will see what advice Seneca has for us once we are thinking clearly, decide that doing right by others is a worthy goal, and form the firm intention of reaching it.

3

JUDGING YOURSELF FAIRLY

Regis quisque intra se animum habet,
ut licentiam sibi dari velit, in se nolit.
(*On Anger* 2.31.3)

3

JUDGING YOURSELF FAIRLY

There is the mind of a monarch within each
of us, wanting to be granted complete
freedom of action but not wanting it to be
turned against us. (*On Anger* 2.31.3)

Treating others fairly obviously depends on
one's view of those others—the subject of
the next chapter—but it also depends, still
more fundamentally, on one's view of oneself: When you come right down to it,
how important are you, and to what does
that importance entitle you? What sort of

person are you, and what sort of person do you want to be?

Now it is clear from the ground we have already covered that Stoicism places enormous emphasis on the care of the self: the mind is, after all, the unique source of the true and final good for each and every one of us, and it is only by clarifying the mind's workings, making them as powerful and consistent as possible, that each of us can advance on the road to wisdom. And yet, somewhat paradoxically, for all the stress that Stoicism places on the self, no ancient philosophical system is more outward turning and other directed.

So the answer to the question "What sort of person do you want to be?" largely depends on the way each of us balances the relation between self and other. And that relation, in turn, is central to a key

Stoic tenet called *oikeiosis* (oy-*kay*-o-sis), "making [something] one's own" (literally, "domesticating"). The term refers to the way that human beings, from birth, develop a sense of self-attachment and self-concern—what we might think of as the "survival instinct"—that causes us to seek what is good for ourselves and to avoid what is bad. At the earliest stages of our lives, we understand what is "good" and what is "bad" only in terms of what helps or hinders us as living creatures: food, shelter, and the like—the "creature comforts"—or their absence. But as we mature, ideally, we should come to understand "good" and "bad" only in terms of what helps or hinders us as rational creatures: wisdom, virtue, a mind attuned to the providential order of the universe—or their absence.

And as we come to this better understanding, the innate impulse to "make
something one's own" should cause us to
regard ever-widening circles of others as ob-
jects of a concern every bit as urgent as our
concern for ourselves: family, community,
country, and—finally, for the truly wise—
all humanity. The key thought here is not so
much "love thy neighbor as thyself," but
rather "consider your neighbor's good to be
as important as your own."

But coming to better understanding is
hard work, and unless we undertake it in
earnest, our innate self-attachment inclines
us to selfish behavior and arrogant ways of
thinking that are the opposite of "large-
minded." As the statement at the head of
this chapter makes clear, Seneca was all too
aware that his main audience—Rome's educated elite, men who were, on average and

(11) Illud praecipue inpedit, quod cito nobis placemus; si invenimus qui nos bonos viros dicat, qui prudentes, qui sanctos, adgnoscimus. Non sumus modica laudatione contenti: quidquid in nos

to a remarkable degree, selfish and arrogant —
would need some coaching, coaxing, and
convincing.

So he urges on his readers several ways to
overcome this innate tendency to think oneself the center of the universe, above all by
cultivating the habit of reflecting on our
dealings with others and practicing the frank
self-assessment that can moderate our sense
of entitlement, the better to avoid the sort
of complacent self-satisfaction that he describes in our first passage.

(11) Here's a particular obstacle: we're
quick to be pleased with ourselves. If we
find someone to say we're good, shrewd,
righteous, we acknowledge the description's truth. We're not satisfied with
measured praise: however thick a flatterer

adulatio sine pudore congessit tamquam debitum prendimus. Optimos nos esse, sapientissimos adfirmantibus adsentimur, cum sciamus illos saepe multa mentiri; adeoque indulgemus nobis ut laudari velimus in id cui contraria cum maxime facimus. Mitissimum ille se in ipsis suppliciis audit, in rapinis liberalissimum et in ebrietatibus ac libidinibus temperantissimum; sequitur itaque ut ideo mutari nolimus quia nos optimos esse credidimus. (12) Alexander cum iam in India vagaretur et gentes ne finitimis quidem satis notas bello vastaret, in obsidione cuiusdam urbis, <dum> circumit muros et inbecillissima moenium quaerit, sagitta ictus diu persedere et incepta agere

shamelessly lays it on, we take it as our due. We agree with those who say we're tip-top and oh-so-wise, though we know they're often terrible liars, and we're so self-indulgent that we want to be praised for behaving in a way that is the opposite of what we are doing at that very moment. Someone hears himself called "most mild" as he metes out punishment, "most generous" in the act of thievery, "most temperate" when he is drunk and whoring: so it follows that we do not want to change, because we believe we are as good as can be. (12) When Alexander was already wandering in India, laying waste to tribes that not even their neighbors knew well, he was circling the walls of some city under siege, looking for the weakest spot. Though struck by an arrow he long pressed on with the siege, but

perseveravit. Deinde cum represso sanguine sicci vulneris dolor cresceret et crus
suspensum equo paulatim obtorpuisset,
coactus absistere "omnes" inquit "iurant
esse me Iovis filium, sed vulnus hoc hominem esse me clamat." (13) Idem nos
faciamus. Pro sua quemque portione
adulatio infatuat: dicamus, "vos quidem
dicitis me prudentem esse, ego autem
video quam multa inutilia concupiscam,
nocitura optem. Ne hoc quidem intellego
quod animalibus satietas monstrat, quis
cibo debeat esse, quis potioni modus;
quantum capiam adhuc nescio." (*Epistle*
59.11–13)

then, with the blood flow stanched, the pain of the wound increased, and his leg slowly became numb as it dangled from his horse: forced to withdraw, he said, "Everyone swears that I am the son of Jupiter, but this wound cries out that I am human." (13) Let's do the same thing. As flattery tries to make us as stupid as it can, let's say, "Sure, you say that I am shrewd, but I know how many useless things I lust for, how many harmful things I pray for. I do not even grasp the limit to be placed on food and drink, something even animals sense when they are full. I still do not know my own limits." (*Epistle* 59.11–13)

Misinterpreting other people's motives and intentions is among the most common causes of unfairness, especially when

(3) Ingenia natura infirma . . . inopia verae iniuriae lascivientia his commoventur, quorum pars maior constat vitio interpretantis. Itaque nec prudentiae quicquam in se esse nec fiduciae ostendit qui contumelia adficitur; non dubie enim contemptum se iudicat, et hic morsus non

self-satisfaction and self-indulgence leave us fundamentally uninterested in others or encourage us to think of them only so far as they serve our own purposes. Cultivating self-awareness counters the sort of "low-mindedness" that sees insult where none is intended and confuses what is merely offensive with what is actually harmful: it is better to model oneself on the wise, whose magnanimity allows them to take in their stride even the sorts of events typically considered major misfortunes:

(3) In the absence of actual injuries . . . a naturally weak character is stirred by imagined slights that mostly arise from an error of interpretation. So those whom an insult affects show that they lack good sense and confidence: they judge that they have been held in contempt, for sure,

sine quadam humilitate animi evenit sup-
primentis se ac descendentis. Sapiens
autem a nullo contemnitur, magnitudi-
nem suam novit nullique tantum de se
licere renuntiat sibi et omnis has, quas
non miserias animorum sed molestias
dixerim, non vincit sed ne sentit quidem.
(4) Alia sunt quae sapientem feriunt,
etiam si non pervertunt, ut dolor corporis
et debilitas aut amicorum liberorumque
amissio et patriae bello flagrantis calamitas: haec non nego sentire sapientem; nec
enim lapidis illi duritiam ferrive adseri-
mus. Nulla virtus est quae non sentias
perpeti. Quid ergo est? quosdam ictus
recipit, sed receptos evincit et sanat et

and this sting is accompanied by a kind of low-mindedness, stifling and demeaning one's self. But no one holds the wise in contempt: they know their own stature and remind themselves that no one has power over them; as for all life's annoyances (I wouldn't call them "troubles"), they don't overcome them—they don't even notice them. (4) There are other things that strike the wise without overwhelming them, like bodily pain and weakness or the loss of friends and children and the misfortune of a homeland ablaze with war: I do not deny that the wise feel these things, for we do not claim that they are hard as rock or iron. It is not a virtue to be impervious to what you must bear. What then? The wise receive blows of a sort but having received them, overcome, allay, and subdue them.

comprimit, haec vero minora ne sentit quidem nec adversus ea solita illa virtute utitur dura tolerandi, sed aut non adnotat aut digna risu putat. (*On the Consistency of the Wise* 10.3–4)

(19) Non quidquid nos offendit et laedit; sed ad rabiem cogunt pervenire deliciae, ut quidquid non ex voluntate respondit iram evocet. (20) Regum nobis induimus animos; nam illi quoque obliti et suarum virium et inbecillitatis alienae sic excandescunt, sic saeviunt, quasi iniuriam acceperint, a cuius rei periculo illos fortunae suae magnitudo tutissimos praestat. Nec hoc ignorant, sed occasionem nocendi

Lesser blows they do not even feel, nor do they deploy against them the virtue that consists of bearing up under hardship: either they do not remark them or they think them laughable. (*On the Consistency of the Wise* 10.3–4)

(19) Not everything that offends us harms us: it is our self-indulgence that drives us wild, provoking rage at whatever does not respond to our wishes. (20) We assume the mindset of royalty, for they too forget their own strength and others' weakness, savagely raging as though they have been injured, though their own great good fortune protects them utterly from the risk of injury. They know this, but still they air their grievances, just looking for the chance to do harm: they

captant querendo; acceperunt iniuriam ut facerent. (*Epistle* 47.19–20)

(9) Facile est . . . occupationes evadere, si occupationum pretia contempseris; illa sunt quae nos morantur et detinent. "Quid ergo? tam magnas spes relinquam? ab ipsa messe discedam? nudum erit latus, incomitata lectica, atrium vacuum?" Ab his ergo inviti homines recedunt et mercedem miseriarum amant,

acknowledge an injury in order to cause one. (*Epistle* 47.19–20)

Because the self-involved aim only at their own satisfaction, the prospect of empty rewards keeps them from understanding where permanent value resides and so from making right choices:

(9) It is easy . . . to escape the cares of public office if you disdain its rewards: those are the things that hold us back and make us linger. "What, then, am I to abandon such great expectations, leave at the very moment of harvest? No guard at my side, no attendant at my litter, my reception hall empty?"[1] People are unwilling to withdraw from these trappings, which they embrace as compensation for their misery while cursing the misery itself.

ipsas execrantur. (10) Sic de ambitione
quomodo de amica queruntur, id est, si
verum adfectum eorum inspicias, non
oderunt sed litigant. Excute istos qui
quae cupiere deplorant et de earum
rerum loquuntur fuga quibus carere non
possunt: videbis voluntariam esse illis in
eo moram quod aegre ferre ipsos et misere
loquuntur. . . . (12) Sed si propter hoc
tergiversaris, ut circumaspicias quantum
feras tecum et quam magna pecunia in-
struas otium, numquam exitum invenies:
nemo cum sarcinis enatat. Emerge ad
meliorem vitam propitiis diis, sed non sic
quomodo istis propitii sunt quibus bono
ac benigno vultu mala magnifica tribue-
runt, ob hoc unum excusati, quod ista

(10) So people complain about ambition as though it were a mistress: if you could see their true feeling, it is not hatred but contrariness. Examine those who bemoan what they have desired and talk about escaping the things they cannot do without: you will see that they linger willingly over what they say makes them wretched and peevish. . . . (12) But if you equivocate, to give yourself time to consider how much cash you might take with you, to provide for your retirement, you will never get away: no one swims clear [of a shipwreck] if he is towing his own baggage. Escape to a better life with the gods' favor—but not the favor they show to those to whom they have given, with a good and kindly countenance, splendid miseries, gifts excused only by the fact that these sources of pain and suffering

quae urunt, quae excruciant, optantibus data sunt. (*Epistle* 22.9–10, 12)

(1) Hae sunt divitiae certae, in quacumque sortis humanae levitate uno loco permansurae, quae quo maiores fuerint, hoc minorem habebunt invidiam. Quid tamquam tuo parcis? Procurator es. (2) Omnia ista quae vos tumidos et supra humana elatos oblivisci cogunt vestrae fragilitatis, quae ferreis claustris custoditis armati, quae ex alieno sanguine rapta vestro defenditis, propter quae classes cruentaturas maria deducitis, propter quae quassatis urbes ignari quantum telorum in aversos fortuna conparet: . . . non sunt

were given in answer to a prayer. (*Epistle* 22.9–10, 12)

(1) [The favors one has freely given] are a kind of wealth, secure, destined to remain in place whatever the vicissitudes of human fortune, the object of less envy the greater they are.[2] Why be stingy as though they were your own possessions? You are just the caretaker. (2) All the things that make people forget their fragility, puffed up and exalted beyond their mere humanity; the things they guard under arms in strongholds of iron, wrested from another's blood and defended with their own; the things that make them launch fleets to stain the sea with blood and shatter cities, unaware of the armaments that fortune readies while their backs are turned: . . . these things are not truly

uestra. In depositi causa sunt iam iamque ad alium dominum spectantia, aut hostis illa aut hostilis animi successor invadet. (3) Quaeris quomodo illa tua facias? Dona dando. Consule igitur rebus tuis et certam tibi earum atque inexpugnabilem possessionem para honestiores illas non solum tutiores facturus. (4) Istud quod suspicis, quo te divitem ac potentem putas, quam diu possides sub nomine sordido iacet: domus est, servus est, nummi sunt. Cum donasti, beneficium est. (*On Benefits* 6.3.1–4)

theirs. They are on deposit and will pass on, any minute now, to another master, whether seized by an enemy or by an heir who thinks like one. (3) Do you ask how to make them your own? Give them as gifts. Take thought for your holdings and render them secure and unassailable by making them more honorable, not just safer. (4) The things you hold in high regard and reckon a source of wealth and power are just lowly bearers of a vulgar name—a house, some cash . . . —as long as you hold onto them. When you give them as gifts, they're acts of kindness. (*On Benefits* 6.3.1–4)

To overcome the excessive sensitivity to injury and insult that self-centeredness breeds, we have to take a step back, to gain the sort of perspective that enables us to understand

(3) . . . Contemnere iniurias et, quas iniuriarum umbras ac suspiciones dixerim, contumelias, ad quas despiciendas non sapiente opus est viro, sed tantum consipiente, qui sibi possit dicere: "utrum merito mihi ista accidunt an inmerito? Si merito, non est contumelia, iudicium est; si inmerito, illi qui iniusta facit erubescendum est." (4) Et quid est illud quod contumelia dicitur? In capitis mei levitatem iocatus est et in oculorum valetudinem et in crurum gracilitatem et in staturam: quae contumelia est quod apparet audire? Coram uno aliquid dictum

ourselves and fairly judge the real force and nature of the things that cause us to be out of sorts:

(3) . . . It does not take a wise person to disdain injuries and insults (the shadows and hints of injuries, I call them) but only someone in their right mind, able to say, "Did that happen to me deservedly or undeservedly? If the former, it is not an insult, it is a judgment; if the latter, the person who behaves unjustly should be ashamed." (4) And what is it that is called an "insult"? Someone made a joke about my baldness, my poor eyesight, my skinny legs, my lack of stature: what sort of insult is it to hear described what's plain to see? We laugh at some remark made before an audience of one; when it is made before a larger audience, we're

ridemus, coram pluribus indignamur, et eorum aliis libertatem non relinquimus quae ipsi in nos dicere adsuevimus. (*On the Consistency of the Wise* 16.3–4)

(9) "Initium est salutis notitia peccati." Egregie mihi hoc dixisse videtur Epicurus; nam qui peccare se nescit corrigi non vult; deprehendas te oportet antequam emendes. (10) Quidam vitiis gloriantur: tu existimas aliquid de remedio cogitare qui mala sua virtutum loco numerant? Ideo quantum

indignant, and we do not grant others the license to say the things we're accustomed to say about ourselves. (*On the Consistency of the Wise* 16.3–4)

And so to develop that capacity for detached reflection Seneca repeatedly urges us to cultivate the habit of regular and systematic self-assessment:

(9) "Awareness of doing wrong is the beginning of well-being." I think that is an outstanding thing that Epicurus said. Whoever does not acknowledge that they have done wrong does not want to be corrected: you must catch yourself out before you make amends. (10) Some people boast about their faults: do you suppose that people who count their wrongdoing as virtue spare a thought

potes te ipse coargue, inquire in te; accu-
satoris primum partibus fungere, deinde
iudicis, novissime deprecatoris; aliquando
te offende. (*Epistle* 28.9–10)

(6) Cum secesseris, non est hoc agendum,
ut de te homines loquantur, sed ut ipse
tecum loquaris. Quid autem loqueris?
quod homines de aliis libentissime faciunt, de te apud te male existima: ad-
suesces et dicere verum et audire. Id
autem maxime tracta quod in te esse in-
firmissimum senties. (7) Nota habet sui
quisque corporis vitia. Itaque alius vo-
mitu levat stomachum, alius frequenti cibo
fulcit, alius interposito ieiunio corpus

about a remedy? Therefore convict yourself of error, to the extent you can, and
look deep within yourself: first play the
part of an accuser, then of a judge, finally
of an intercessor. Sometimes, offend
yourself. (*Epistle* 28.9–10)

(6) When you have retired [from public
life], the aim is not that people should talk
about you, but that you should talk with
yourself. What will you say? What people
very happily say behind others' backs—
judge yourself harshly, to your face. You
will get used to speaking and hearing the
truth. And address especially what you
take to be your weakest points. (7) Everyone knows their own bodies' flaws. Accordingly one person relieves his stomach
by vomiting, another fortifies it with frequent meals, another drains and cleanses

exhaurit et purgat; ii quorum pedes dolor repetit aut vino aut balineo abstinent: in cetera neglegentes huic a quo saepe infestantur occurrunt. Sic in animo nostro sunt quaedam quasi causariae partes quibus adhibenda curatio est. (8) Quid in otio facio? ulcus meum curo. Si ostenderem tibi pedem turgidum, lividam manum, aut contracti cruris aridos nervos, permitteres mihi uno loco iacere et fovere morbum meum: maius malum est hoc, quod non possum tibi ostendere: in pectore ipso collectio et vomica est. (*Epistle* 68.6–8)

Faciam ergo quod iubes, et quid agam et quo ordine libenter tibi scribam. Observabo me protinus et, quod est utilissimum, diem meum recognoscam. Hoc

his body with fasting. People with recurrent gout abstain from wine or bathing: though careless in other regards, they counteract the thing that often attacks them. So in our mind there are, so to speak, diseased regions to which a course of treatment must be applied. (8) What do I do in retirement? I attend to my own wound. If I were to show you a swollen foot, a bruised hand, the shrunken sinews of a withered leg, you'd allow me to lie in one place and relieve my illness. This is a greater woe, one I cannot show you: there is an abscess in my heart. (*Epistle* 68.6–8)

I will do, then, what you bid, and gladly describe what I am doing and in what order. I will keep a watch on myself straightway and—the most useful step—review my day. The fact that we do not

nos pessimos facit, quod nemo vitam suam respicit; quid facturi simus cogitamus, et id raro, quid fecerimus non cogitamus; atqui consilium futuri ex praeterito venit. (*Epistle* 83.2)

look back over our lives makes us worse. We ponder—though rarely—what we are to do, but we do not ponder at all what we have done—and yet planning for the future depends on the past. (*Epistle* 83.2)

Seneca in fact practiced what he preached, as he tells us near the end of his treatise *On Anger*, where he describes the minute end-of-the-day review that he conducts when he retires each night. He is particularly concerned to root out the causes of anger, but the exercise can easily be broadened to include the causes of unfairness in speech and action. Most of the circumstances he describes seem quite as current and familiar as the folly of arguing with strangers on the internet:

36 (2) Desinet ira et moderatior erit quae sciet sibi cotidie ad iudicem esse veniendum. Quicquam ergo pulchrius hac consuetudine excutiendi totum diem? Qualis ille somnus post recognitionem sui sequitur, quam tranquillus, quam altus ac liber, cum aut laudatus est animus aut admonitus et speculator sui censorque secretus cognovit de moribus suis! (3) Vtor hac potestate et cotidie apud me causam dico. Cum sublatum e conspectu lumen est et conticuit uxor moris iam mei conscia, totum diem meum scrutor factaque ac dicta mea remetior; nihil mihi ipse abscondo, nihil transeo. Quare enim quicquam ex erroribus meis timeam, cum

36 (2) Your anger will cease and become more controllable if it knows that every day it must come before a judge. Is there anything finer, then, than this habit of scrutinizing the entire day? What fine sleep follows this self-examination—how peaceful, how deep and free, when the mind has been either praised or admonished, when the sentinel and secret censor of the self has conducted its inquiry into one's own character! (3) I exercise this jurisdiction daily and plead my case before myself. When the light has been removed and my wife has fallen silent, aware of this habit that's now mine, I examine my entire day and go back over what I have done and said, hiding nothing from myself, passing nothing by. For why should I fear any consequence from my mistakes,

possim dicere: "vide ne istud amplius facias, nunc tibi ignosco.

(4) "In illa disputatione pugnacius lo-
cutus es: noli postea congredi cum im-
peritis; nolunt discere qui numquam
didicerunt. Illum liberius admonuisti quam
debebas, itaque non emendasti sed of-
fendisti: de cetero vide, [ne] non tantum
an verum sit quod dicis, sed an ille cui
dicitur veri patiens sit: admoneri bonus
gaudet, pessimus quisque rectorem asper-
rime patitur.

37 (1) "In convivio quorundam te sales
et in dolorem tuum iacta uerba teti-
gerunt: vitare vulgares convictus memento;

when I am able to say, "See that you do not do it again—but now I forgive you.

(4) "In that discussion you spoke too aggressively: from now on steer clear of people who don't know what they're talking about. People who have never learned do not want to learn. You admonished that fellow more candidly than you should, and as a result you didn't correct him, you offended him: in future consider not just whether what you say is true but whether the person you are talking to can take the truth. A good man delights in being admonished, but the worst people have the hardest time enduring correction.

37 (1) "At that banquet certain people's witty remarks, and words bandied about to bruise you, got under your skin, so remember to avoid unrefined gatherings:

solutior est post vinum licentia, quia ne
sobriis quidem pudor est. (2) Iratum
vidisti amicum tuum ostiario causidici
alicuius aut divitis quod intrantem sum-
moverat, et ipse pro illo iratus extremo
mancipio fuisti: irasceris ergo catenario
cani? et hic, cum multum latravit, obiecto
cibo mansuescit. (3) Recede longius et
ride! Nunc iste se aliquem putat quod cus-
todit litigatorum turba limen obsessum;
nunc ille qui intra iacet felix fortuna-
tusque est et beati hominis iudicat ac po-
tentis indicium difficilem ianuam: nescit

because people in such places have no sense of shame even when they are sober, their idea of what is permissible is still more relaxed after they have been drinking. (2) You saw your friend become angry with some lawyer's or rich man's doorkeeper because he thrust him aside as he was entering, and you yourself were angry with that utterly low creature on his behalf: will you become angry, then, with a chained dog? And a dog, after it has had a good bark, becomes gentle when you toss it a treat. (3) Stand back a bit farther and laugh! That fellow thinks he is someone now because he keeps watch over a threshold thronged by people pursuing lawsuits; the man who now reclines within prospers as fortune's favorite and thinks a door that is hard to enter is the mark of a rich and powerful

durissimum esse ostium carceris. Prae-
sume animo multa tibi esse patienda:
numquis se hieme algere miratur, numquis in mari nausiare, in via concuti?
Fortis est animus ad quae praeparatus
venit. (4) Minus honorato loco positus
irasci coepisti convivatori, vocatori,
ipsi qui tibi praeferebatur: demens, quid
interest quam lecti premas partem? ho-
nestiorem te aut turpiorem potest facere
pulvinus? (5) Non aequis quendam oculis vidisti, quia de ingenio tuo male lo-
cutus est: recipis hanc legem? Ergo te
Ennius, quo non delectaris, odisset et

fellow. He does not know that the hard-est door is the prison door. Anticipate that you must put up with many things: no one is astonished that he is cold in winter, is he? or seasick on the sea, or shoved in the street? The mind faces bravely the things it is prepared to en-counter. (4) Assigned a place of less dis-tinction you began to become angry with your fellow guest, with the man who in-vited you, and with the man who was given preference over you:[3] madman, what difference does it make on what part of the couch you plant your weight? Can a pillow make you more honorable or more shameful? (5) You gave someone a dirty look because he spoke ill of your talent: do you accept this as a principle of behavior? Then Ennius, in whom you take no pleasure, would have hated you,

Hortensius simultates tibi indiceret et Cicero, si derideres carmina eius, inimicus esset." (*On Anger* 3.36.2–37.5)

and Hortensius would quarrel with you, and Cicero, were you to mock his poetry, would be your enemy."[4] (*On Anger* 3.36.2–37.5)

Accurately assessing your behavior in this way is obviously indispensable to answering the questions with which this chapter began: what sort of person are you, and what sort of person do you want to be? It is also indispensable to answering the question taken up in the next chapter: how can you best be certain to do right by others?

4

DOING RIGHT BY OTHERS

Totum hoc quo continemur et unum est et
deus: et socii sumus eius et membra.
(*Epistle* 92.30)

4

DOING RIGHT BY OTHERS

This totality by which we are embraced is a
single, constant whole, and it is God: we
are God's comrades and God's limbs.
(*Epistle* 92.30)

Two important aspects of Stoicism provide
a useful prelude to this chapter. The first is
hinted at by the quotation above: we are all
"God's limbs." The entire universe, the Stoics held, is composed of matter, without
vacuum or void. Some of this matter is large
and visible, while much of it is unimagin-
ably fine and invisible. One example of the

latter sort of matter is the air we breathe; another example—a finer sort of matter still—is the divine reason that permeates the universe, giving it its shape, order, and providential purpose and setting it in motion.[1] And the infinitely fine matter that constitutes the divine reason—which the Stoics also called "God"—is identical to and continuous with the matter that constitutes the reason that human beings, alone of all animals, share with God. Long story short, all human beings are literally, physically, materially connected with God and with each other, as our fingers are connected to our hands and our limbs are connected to our bodies (the analogies are the Stoics'). This view of the universe's materiality, and the interconnectedness of all being as "a single, constant whole," is the physical foundation for the ethical doctrine of *oikeiosis*

encountered in the previous chapter: the wise come to regard the good of all others as indistinguishable from their own because they understand that we are in fact all parts of an integrated whole.

The second point to bear in mind is this: Stoicism always operates with a binocular view of what it means to be human. On the one hand, there is the core belief that we are all built by nature to be capable of virtue and to live the best sort of human life—in fact, as we have seen, we are built by nature to be capable of acting with the mind of a god, minus the immortality. On the other hand, there is the awareness that—because our intellectual development is stunted, and because we are distracted or corrupted by the culture that surrounds us—just about all of us, just about every day, betray our natural capacities and behave like fools. Doing

right by others requires us to act on the core belief in guiding our own intentions and actions as we strive for virtue, while using the latter awareness to calibrate our views of others and, whenever possible, to cut them some slack. Much of the advice we saw in the last chapter, on getting a clear view of ourselves, concerned our own striving for virtue. Much of the advice that we will see Seneca give in what follows falls under the heading "cutting some slack."

That we almost inevitably fall short of the moral perfection that is naturally within our grasp can give Stoicism a tragic tinge. But Seneca urges us not to succumb to tragedy. Instead, when we are confronted by human foibles and failings, we should follow the recommendation of the philosopher Democritus: stand back and laugh.

(2) In hoc . . . flectendi sumus, ut omnia vulgi vitia non invisa nobis sed ridicula videantur et Democritum potius imitemur quam Heraclitum. Hic enim, quotiens in publicum processerat, flebat, ille ridebat, huic omnia quae agimus miseriae, illi ineptiae videbantur. Elevanda ergo omnia et facili animo ferenda: humanius est deridere vitam quam deplorare. (3) Adice quod de humano quoque genere melius meretur qui ridet illud quam qui luget: ille ei spei bonae aliquid relinquit, hic autem stulte deflet quae corrigi posse desperat; et universa contemplanti maioris animi est qui risum non tenet quam qui lacrimas, quando lenissimum adfectum animi movet et nihil magnum, nihil

(2) We should bring ourselves to see that all of humanity's common faults are not hateful but laughable, and to imitate Democritus rather than Heraclitus.[2] Whenever the latter went among the people, he wept, seeing wretchedness in all we do; the former laughed at the foolishness he saw. We should make light of it all and bear it indulgently: laughing at the way we live is more humane than lamenting. (3) Add that the person who laughs serves the human race better than the one who grieves: the one gives it reason to hope, the other foolishly deplores what he despairs of seeing made better. And if one takes a general view, a person who cannot restrain his laughter is more large-minded than the one who cannot restrain his tears, since laughter stirs the mildest emotion and does not reckon that

severum, ne miserum quidem ex tanto paratu putat. (*On Tranquility of Mind* 15.2–3)

6 (1) Cogitato, in hac civitate, in qua turba per latissima itinera sine intermissione defluens eliditur, quotiens aliquid obstitit, quod cursum eius velut torrentis rapidi moraretur, in qua tribus eodem tempore theatris caveae postulantur, in qua consumitur, quidquid terris omnibus aratur, quanta solitudo ac vastitas futura sit, si nihil relinquitur, nisi quod iudex severus absolverit. (2) Quotus quisque ex quaesitoribus est, qui non ex ipsa ea lege

anything consequential, serious, or even unhappy derives from life's great pageant. (*On Tranquility of Mind* 15.2–3)

By understanding human weakness, we come to understand that none of us is innocent: we should therefore judge others as we would want to be judged.

6 (1) In this community—where crowds in ceaseless motion on the broadest streets get jammed whenever an obstacle slows their torrential flow, where access is needed to three theaters at the same time, where all the produce of the world's farms is consumed—imagine what a great and lonely desolation there would be if there remained only the fraction whom a strict judge might acquit. (2) How rare is the judge who would not be held liable by

teneatur, qua quaerit? quotus quisque accusator vacat culpa? Et nescio, an nemo ad dandam veniam difficilior sit, quam qui illam petere saepius meruit. (3) Peccavimus omnes, alii gravia, alii leviora, alii ex destinato, alii forte inpulsi aut aliena nequitia ablati; alii in bonis consiliis parum fortiter stetimus et innocentiam inviti ac retinentes perdidimus; nec deliquimus tantum, sed usque ad extremum aevi delinquemus. . . .

17 (1) Nullum animal morosius est, nullum maiore arte tractandum quam homo, nulli magis parcendum. Quid enim est stultius quam in iumentis quidem et

the very court over which he presides? How rare is the blameless accuser? And probably no one is more resistant when it comes to granting pardon than one who has too often deserved to seek it. (3) We have all done wrong, some more gravely, others more trivially, some intentionally, others acting on random impulse or led astray by another's wickedness; some of us have been too little steadfast in standing by our good intentions and have lost our innocence unwillingly and reluctantly. And not only have we fallen short, but we will continue to fall short to the end of our days. . . .

17 (1) No animal is more cross-grained or requires more skillful handling than a human being, and none stands in greater need of forbearance. For what could be more foolish than to blush at becoming

canibus erubescere iras exercere, pessima autem condicione sub \<homine\> homi- nem esse? Morbis medemur nec irascimur; atqui et hic morbus est animi; mollem medicinam desiderat ipsumque medentem minime infestum aegro. (*On Mercy* 1.6.1– 3, 17.1)

"Plus accipere debui, sed illi facile non fuit plus dare, in multos dividenda liberalitas erat." "Hoc initium est, boni consulamus et animum eius grate excipiendo evoce- mus." "Parum fecit sed saepius faciet." "Illum mihi praetulit—et me multis." "Ille

angry at mules and dogs, but to want to subject one human being to another on the worst possible terms? We treat diseases without anger, and yet this is a disease of the mind, requiring not just gentle treatment but also a healer who is in no way hostile to the patient. (*On Mercy* 1.6.1–3, 17.1)

Judging others fairly starts with trying to understand their intentions and, in so doing, giving them the benefit of the doubt:

"I deserved more—but he could not easily give it, he had to apportion his generosity among many."[3] "This is a start—let's be satisfied and by our gratitude encourage him to do more." "It was too little—but there will be more installments." "He preferred that person

non est mihi par virtutibus nec officiis sed
habuit suam Venerem; querendo non
efficiam ut maioribus dignus sim sed ut
datis indignus." "Plura illis hominibus tur-
pissimis data sunt. Quid ad rem? Quam
raro fortuna iudicat!" (*On Benefits* 2.28.2)

(2) Nemo dicit sibi, "hoc propter quod
irascor aut feci aut fecisse potui"; nemo
animum facientis sed ipsum aestimat factum: atqui ille intuendus est, voluerit an
inciderit, coactus sit an deceptus, odium
secutus sit an praemium, sibi morem ges-
serit an manum alteri commodaverit.
Aliquid aetas peccantis facit, aliquid

to me—and me to many." "I am a better person and more dutiful—but [the one he favored] has his own charm, and complaining will make me unworthy of what I got, not worthy of getting more." "More did go to those utterly shameful characters—but so what? Luck very rarely shows good judgment." (*On Benefits* 2.28.2)

(2) No one says to himself, "This thing that is making me angry—either I have done it myself, or I could have." No one gauges the other's intention, only the act itself. Yet it's the agent we ought to consider: was his act voluntary or accidental, was she compelled or deceived, was he motivated by hatred or a reward, did she gratify herself or serve another? The wrongdoers' age should be taken into

fortuna, ut ferre ac pati aut humanum sit
aut utile. (3) Eo nos loco constituamus
quo ille est cui irascimur: nunc facit nos
iracundos iniqua nostri aestimatio et
quae facere vellemus pati nolumus. (*On
Anger* 3.12.2–3)

(1) Num quid est iniquius homine qui
eum odit a quo in turba calcatus aut res-
persus aut quo nollet impulsus est? . . .
Quid est aliud quod illum querellae exi-
mat, cum in re sit iniuria, quam nescisse
quid faceret? (2) Eadem res efficit ne hic
beneficium dederit, ne ille iniuriam fecerit: et amicum et inimicum voluntas

account, and also their fortune, making forbearance a matter of either kindness or expediency. (3) Let's put ourselves in the place of the person with whom we are angry: from that perspective we see that valuing ourselves unfairly makes us angry, and that we are unwilling to tolerate an act that we would willingly commit. (*On Anger* 3.12.2–3)

(1) What is more unfair than hating someone who stepped on your foot in a crowd, or splashed you or shoved you in a direction you did not want to take? . . . When an injury is at issue, the fact that people did not know what they were doing is the very thing that exculpates them. (2) The same consideration nullifies both a favor and an injury: it is the intention that makes one a friend or an enemy.

facit. Quam multos militiae morbus eripuit! Quosdam ne ad ruinam domus suae occurrerent inimicus vadimonio tenuit, ne in piratarum manus pervenirent quidam naufragio consecuti sunt: nec huic tamen beneficium debemus, quia extra sensum officii casus est, nec inimico cuius nos lis servavit dum vexat ac detinet. (*On Benefits* 6.9.1–2)

Non vertit omnia in peius nec quaerit cui inputet casum, et peccata hominum ad fortunam potius refert. Non calumniatur verba nec vultus; quidquid accidit benigne interpretando levat. Non offensae potius quam offici meminit; quantum

How many has sickness rescued from military service! Some people have avoided being at home when their house collapsed because an enemy forced them to appear in court, while others have escaped pirates by being shipwrecked: we owe a favor neither to the wreck, since acts of chance are not motivated by a sense of duty, nor to the enemy whose suit saved us with its delays and vexations. (*On Benefits* 6.9.1–2)

[The wise] do not take everything at its worst or look for someone to blame; they rather attribute people's mistakes to misfortune. They do not criticize words and looks unfairly but mitigate whatever happens by interpreting it kindly. They do not recall offensive behavior more tenaciously than the dutiful sort; to the extent

potest in priore ac meliore se memoria
detinet, nec mutat animum adversus bene
meritos nisi multum male facta praece-
dunt et manifestum etiam coniventi dis-
crimen est; tunc quoque in hoc dumtaxat,
ut talis sit post maiorem iniuriam qualis
ante beneficium. Nam cum beneficio par
est iniuria, aliquid in animo benivolentiae
remanet. (*Epistle* 81.25)

possible they dwell on prior, better behavior and do not change their attitude
toward deserving people until many bad
acts intervene and the difference is clear
even to one turning a blind eye—and even
then their attitude is the same after being
wronged as it was before being benefited.
For when the wrong and the benefit are
of the same weight, some kindly feeling
abides. (*Epistle* 81.25)

Just as the fact that we have intentions ex-
pressible in words is a distinguishing trait of
human beings, so the fact that we can pre-
sume to understand the intentions of others,
even when not expressed in words, is a gift
that we owe to our shared humanity—a
bond on which we should, like the Stoics,
place the highest value.

Nefas est nocere patriae; ergo civi quoque, nam hic pars patriae est—sanctae partes sunt, si universum venerabile est; ergo et homini, nam hic in maiore tibi urbe civis est. Quid si nocere velint manus pedibus, manibus oculi? Vt omnia inter se membra consentiunt quia singula servari totius interest, ita homines singulis parcent quia ad coetum geniti sunt, salva autem esse societas nisi custodia et amore partium non potest. (*On Anger* 2.31.7)

It is unspeakably wrong to harm one's homeland; therefore, it is unspeakably wrong to harm fellow-citizens, too, for they are part of the homeland—the parts are sacrosanct if the whole is worthy of our worship. Therefore it is unspeakably wrong to harm human beings too, for they are your fellow citizens in the cosmopolis.[4] What if the hands wanted to harm the feet, the eyes the hands? As all our limbs are in harmony because it is best for the whole that the individual parts be protected, so human beings will spare each individual because they have been born to form a social union, and a society cannot be sound save through the affectionate protection of its parts. (*On Anger* 2.31.7)

(3) "Ego terras omnis tamquam meas videbo, meas tamquam omnium. Ego sic vivam quasi sciam aliis esse me natum et naturae rerum hoc nomine gratias agam: quo enim melius genere negotium meum agere potuit? unum me donavit omnibus, uni mihi omnis. . . . (5) . . . Ero amicis iucundus, inimicis mitis et facilis. Exorabor antequam roger, et honestis precibus occurram. Patriam meam esse mundum sciam et praesides deos, hos supra me circaque me stare factorum dictorumque censores. Quandoque aut natura spiritum repetet aut ratio dimittet, testatus exibo bonam me conscientiam amasse, bona studia, nullius per me libertatem deminutam, minime meam"–qui haec facere

(3) "I will view all lands as my own, my own as belonging to all. I will live as if aware that I was born for others and thank the universe on that account: how could it have done better by me? It gave me, one individual, as a gift to all people, and all people to me.... (5)... My friends will find me congenial, my enemies mild and accommodating. I will be won over before I am asked and hasten to meet all honorable requests. I will know that the world is my homeland, the gods its guardians, standing above and around me as judges of my words and deeds. Whenever nature asks for my spirit back or reason lets it go,[5] I will depart with an oath that I have loved a good conscience and honorable pursuits, and that I diminished no one's freedom, least of all my own": those who make this their goal,

proponet, volet, temptabit, ad deos iter faciet." (*On the Happy Life* 20.3, 5)

(2) Nec potest quisquam beate degere qui se tantum intuetur, qui omnia ad utilitates suas convertit: alteri vivas oportet, si vis tibi vivere. (3) Haec societas diligenter et sancte observata, quae nos homines hominibus miscet et iudicat aliquod esse commune ius generis humani. (*Epistle* 48.2–3)

their intention, the object of their striving, will journey to the gods. (*On the Happy Life* 20.3, 5)

(2) People who have regard only for themselves and turn everything to their own advantage cannot live the best human life: you must live for others if you want to live for yourself. (3) If maintained carefully and faithfully, this principle makes us all each other's partners and establishes a shared standard of right for the human race. (*Epistle* 48.2–3)

The Stoics held not just that virtue is its own reward but that virtue is the only reward worth seeking for its own sake, as an end in itself. Just so, since treating others fairly is a virtue, it is worth practicing fairness for its own sake, just with the aim of doing right.

.

(1) Quid est quare grati velimus esse cum morimur, quare singulorum perpendamus officia, quare id agamus in omnem vitam nostram memoria decurrente ne cuius officii videamur obliti? Nihil iam superest quo spes porrigatur, in illo tamen cardine positi abire e rebus humanis quam gratissimi volumus. (2) Est videlicet magna in ipso opere merces rei et ad adliciendas mentes hominum ingens honesti

In these passages Seneca illustrates the point, first through a central institution of Roman life—making wills in which friends are gratefully remembered—and then through a metaphor—of playing ball—borrowed from the great Stoic philosopher Chrysippus (280?–207 BCE):

(1) Why do we want to express our gratitude as we die? Why do we so carefully weigh individuals' dutiful behavior, letting our memory traverse our lives' whole course, lest we appear forgetful of how we have been obliged? We hold out no hope for further gain, yet when we're poised on that turning point we want to pass from human concerns with the fullest expression of our gratitude. (2) Plainly, there is a reward in the very effort, and in the vast power of honorable behavior to

potentia, cuius pulchritudo animos cir-
cumfundit et delenitos admiratione lu-
minis ac fulgoris sui rapit. (*On Benefits*
4.22.1–2)

(3) Volo Chrysippi nostri uti similitudine
de pilae lusu, quam cadere non est du-
bium aut mittentis vitio aut excipientis:
tum cursum suum servat ubi inter manus
utriusque apte ab utroque et iactata et ex-
cepta versatur; necesse est autem lusor
bonus aliter illam conlusori longo, aliter
brevi mittat. Eadem beneficii ratio est:
nisi utrique personae, dantis et accipien-
tis, aptatur, nec ab hoc exibit nec ad illum
perveniet ut debet. (4) Si cum exercitato
et docto negotium est, audacius pilam

win over people's sentiments: its beauty enfolds our minds and ravishes them as they are soothed by the wonder of its brilliant light. (*On Benefits* 4.22.1–2)

(3) I want to use Chrysippus's metaphor of a ball game, which, we know, is ended when either server or receiver makes a mistake:[6] the ball maintains its proper course when it goes back and forth from one player to the other as it is put in play and received. Inevitably, moreover, a good player serves the ball one way to a tall partner, another way to a short one. A benefit follows the same principle: unless it is attuned to the characters of the benefactor and the recipient, it will not pass from the one or reach the other as it should. (4) If we are dealing with a skilled and experienced player, we use a more

mittemus: utcumque enim venerit, manus illam expedita et agilis repercutiet. Si cum tirone et indocto, non tam rigide nec tam excusse sed languidius et in ipsam eius derigentes manum remissae occurremus. Idem faciendum est in beneficiis: quosdam doceamus et satis iudicemus si conantur, si audent, si volunt. (*On Benefits* 2.17.3–4)

(31) Doce me quam sacra res sit iustitia alienum bonum spectans, nihil ex se

spirited serve: however it arrives, it will be patted back with a free and nimble hand. If the other is an unskilled novice, we will not meet the ball so briskly and smartly when it is returned but guide it back more gently to the other's very hand. We should do the same in the case of favors: we should teach some people and judge it enough if they make the attempt [to return] boldly and willingly. (*On Benefits* 2.17.3–4)

In such common, everyday ways, we cultivate "the fairness that looks to another's good" and so try to treat others as we would want the providential God to treat us.

(31) Teach me what a sacred thing is the fairness that looks to another's good, seeking only to be of service, having no

petens nisi usum sui. Nihil sit illi cum ambitione famaque: sibi placeat. Hoc ante omnia sibi quisque persuadeat: me iustum esse gratis oportet. Parum est. Adhuc illud persuadeat sibi: me in hanc pulcherrimam virtutem ultro etiam inpendere iuvet; tota cogitatio a privatis commodis quam longissime aversa sit. Non est quod spectes quod sit iustae rei praemium: maius in iusto est. (32) Illud adhuc tibi adfige . . . nihil ad rem pertinere quam multi aequitatem tuam noverint. Qui virtutem suam publicari vult non virtuti laborat sed gloriae. Non vis esse iustus sine gloria? at mehercules saepe iustus esse debebis cum infamia, et tunc, si sapis, mala opinio bene parta delectet. (*Epistle* 113.31–32)

truck with ambition and fame, content with itself. Let us each be convinced of this above all: it is right to be fair without reward. But that is too little: let us each be further persuaded even to take pleasure in this most beautiful virtue at a cost to ourselves, with all our thoughts removed as far as possible from personal advantage. There is no reason to consider what a fair reward for fair behavior might be: the greater reward lies in fairness itself. (32) Keep fixed in your mind . . . that it is irrelevant whether many know of your fairness. Those who want their virtue publicized toil for glory's sake, not virtue's. You do not want to be fair without fame? Good grief, you will often have to be fair at the cost of infamy—and then, if you are wise, a bad name honorably won will delight you. (*Epistle* 113.31–32)

(1) Quoniam deorum feci mentionem, optime hoc exemplum principi constituam ad quod formetur, ut se talem esse civibus quales sibi deos velit. Expedit ergo habere inexorabilia peccatis atque erroribus numina, expedit usque ad ultimam infesta perniciem? Et quis regum erit tutus? Cuius non membra haruspices colligent? (2) Quod si di placabiles et aequi delicta potentium non statim fulminibus persequuntur, quanto aequius est hominem hominibus praepositum miti animo exercere imperium et cogitare uter mundi status gratior oculis pulchriorque sit, sereno et puro die, an cum fragoribus crebris omnia quatiuntur et

(1) Since I've mentioned the gods, I might best set down this model for a prince to imitate:[7] let him wish to treat his fellow citizens as he wishes the gods to treat him. Is it in our interest, then, for the powers above to be implacable when we do wrong and go astray, for their hostility to extend to our utter destruction? Indeed, what king will be safe; whose limbs would the soothsayers not gather?[8] (2) But if the gods, fair and easily appeased as they are, do not immediately punish misdeeds of the powerful with lightning blasts, how much fairer is it for the one human being set in charge of the rest to exercise his power mildly, and to ponder whether the state of the world is more attractive and pleasing when the sky is clear, the sun shining, or when repeated peals of thunder shake all creation and lightning bolts

ignes hinc atque illinc micant! Atqui non
alia facies est quieti moratique imperii
quam sereni caeli et nitentis. (*On Mercy*
1.7.1–2)

Non est autem quod tardiores faciat ad
bene merendum turba ingratorum. . . .
Ne deos quidem inmortales ab hac tam
effusa nec cess<ante benign>itate sacrilegi
neglegentesque eorum deterrent: utuntur
natura sua et cuncta interque illa ipsos
munerum suorum malos interpretes
iuvant. Hos sequamur duces, quantum
humana inbecillitas patitur. (*On Benefits*
1.1.9)

blaze from every quarter! Yet the calm and deliberate exercise of power has exactly the same appearance as a clear and brilliant sky. (*On Mercy* 1.7.1–2)

There is, finally, no better model for doing right by others than the God (or gods)[9] whose goodwill is constant and complete, and whose perfect beneficence Seneca tries again and again to convey.

There is no reason why a throng of ingrates should discourage us from being of service.... Not even the immortal gods are deterred from being extravagantly and ceaselessly kind by people who abuse or neglect them: they put their own nature to work by aiding all the world, including those who misinterpret their gifts. (*On Benefits* 1.1.9)

(1) Propositum est nobis secundum rerum naturam vivere et deorum exemplum sequi. Di autem, quodcumque faciunt, in eo quid praeter ipsam faciendi rationem secuntur—nisi forte illos existimas fructum operum suorum ex fumo extorum et turis odore percipere? (2) Vide quanta cottidie moliantur, quanta distribuant, quantis terras fructibus impleant. . . . Omnia ista sine mercede, sine ullo ad ipsos perveniente commodo faciunt. (3) Hoc nostra quoque ratio, si ab exemplari suo non aberrat, servet, ne ad res honestas conducta veniat. Pudeat ullum venale esse beneficium: gratuitos habemus deos. (*On Benefits* 4.25.1–3)

(2) Ad illa itaque cogitationes tuas flecte: "Non est relata mihi gratia: quid faciam?"

(1) It is our goal to live according to nature and model ourselves on the gods. But what rationale do the gods have for all they do beyond the very doing—unless you suppose, perhaps, that they receive the smoke of sacrifice and the whiff of incense as a reward for their works? (2) Consider all they do every day, all they dispense, all the fruits with which they stock the earth. . . . They do all this without compensation, with no advantage accruing. (3) If we do not stray from our models, let human reason also preserve this principle: honorable behavior is not for hire. Any favor we do for a price should be a cause of shame: we have the gods for free. (*On Benefits* 4.25.1–3)

(2) Turn your thoughts to this matter too: "I received no thanks: what am I to do?"

Quod di, omnium rerum optimi auctores, qui beneficia ignorantibus dare incipiunt, ingratis perseverant. . . . (4) . . . More optimorum parentium, qui maledictis suorum infantium adrident, non cessant di beneficia congerere de beneficiorum auctore dubitantibus, sed aequali tenore bona sua per gentes populosque distribuunt; unam potentiam, prodesse, sortiti spargunt oportunis imbribus terras, maria flatu movent, siderum cursu notant tempora. . . . (5) Imitemur illos: demus etiam si multa <in> inritum data sunt. (*On Benefits* 7.31.2, 4–5)

(10) Parem autem te deo pecunia non faciet: deus nihil habet. Praetexta non faciet:

What the gods do — those best authors of all things — who begin by benefiting those who are unaware of them and continue by benefiting the ungrateful. . . . (4) Like the best parents, who smile when abused by their small children, the gods ceaselessly heap up benefits for people skeptical of the benefits' source, distributing their goods throughout nations and peoples, their course unchanged. Allotted one power only — that of doing good — they sprinkle the lands with well-timed showers, stir the seas with the winds, mark the seasons by the stars' course. . . . (5) We should imitate them: we should give even if much is given in vain. (*On Benefits* 7.31.2, 4–5)

(10) Money will not make you equal to God: God has none. Neither will a robe

deus nudus est. Fama non faciet nec osten-
tatio tui et in populos nominis dimissa
notitia: nemo novit deum, multi de illo
male existimant, et inpune. Non turba ser-
vorum lecticam tuam per itinera urbana ac
peregrina portantium: deus ille maximus
potentissimusque ipse vehit omnia. Ne
forma quidem et vires beatum te facere
possunt: nihil horum patitur vetustatem.
(11) Quaerendum est quod non fiat in dies
peius, cui non possit obstari. Quid hoc
est? animus, sed hic rectus, bonus, magnus. Quid aliud voces hunc quam deum in
corpore humano hospitantem? Hic animus tam in equitem Romanum quam in
libertinum, quam in servum potest cadere.
Quid est enim eques Romanus aut liberti-
nus aut servus? nomina ex ambitione aut

of office:[10] God is naked. Neither will
fame or self-display or far-flung notori-
ety: no one knows God; many judge God
unfairly, with impunity. A throng of por-
ters carrying your litter through Rome's
byways or abroad will not do it: God, the
greatest and most powerful, carries all.
Not even beauty and strength can make
you live the best life: nothing of these
survives for long. (11) You must ask what
does not become worse each day, what
overcomes every obstacle. What is it? The
mind, provided it is upright, good, and
great. What else would you call this mind
save God at home in a human body. This
mind is as fitting for a Roman knight as
it is for a freedman or one enslaved. For
what are "knight" or "freedman" or
"slave" but labels deriving from ambition
or wrongdoing? It is possible to leap up

iniuria nata. Subsilire in caelum ex angulo licet. (*Epistle* 31.10–11)

(14) Iuppiter omnia habet, sed nempe aliis tradidit habenda: ad ipsum hic unus usus pertinet, quod utendi omnibus causa est: sapiens tam aequo animo omnia apud alios videt contemnitque quam Iuppiter et hoc se magis suspicit quod Iuppiter uti illis non potest, sapiens non vult. (15) Credamus itaque Sextio monstranti pulcherrimum iter et clamanti "hac itur ad astra, hac secundum frugalitatem, hac secundum temperantiam, hac secundum fortitudinem." Non sunt dii fastidiosi, non invidi: admittunt et ascendentibus manum porrigunt. (*Epistle* 73.14–15)

to heaven from a lowly nook.[11] (*Epistle* 31.10–11)

(14) Jupiter possesses all things, granted, but he has passed them along for others to possess: he himself uses them only in causing all others to use them. With the equanimity of Jupiter, the wise see others possess everything and care not; they esteem themselves the more because while Jupiter is unable to use those things, they have no desire to use them. (15) So let's trust in Sextius as he shows us the fairest path and exclaims, "This is the way to the stars, the way of thrift, of moderation, of fortitude."[12] The gods are not disdainful or begrudging: they open the door and give a helping hand to those making the ascent. (*Epistle* 73.14–15)

5

BEING MERCIFUL

Illud ante omnia cogita, foedam esse et execrabilem vim nocendi et alienissimam homini. (*On Anger* 2.31.6)

Clementia omnibus quidem hominibus secundum naturam. (*On Mercy* 1.5.2)

5

BEING MERCIFUL

Consider this above all: the power to harm is disgusting and detestable, and utterly alien to a human being. (*On Anger* 2.31.6)

Mercy is natural for all human beings. (*On Mercy* 1.5.2)

Taken literally, elements of both statements just above might raise an eyebrow or two. But in speaking of what is "alien" to humans and what is "natural," Seneca of course did not mean that human beings lack the capacity to do harm or that they practice mercy in the same unthinking way in which they

breathe. He meant that being merciful is in accordance with—and doing harm is contrary to—the way that providential Nature constructed us as human beings: a person who behaved only and exactly as Nature intended—which is to say, as God intended—would never do harm and would always be merciful, bestowing the human good that Seneca explores in his essay *On Mercy*, addressed to the eighteen-year-old emperor Nero.[1] Because it considers its subject from the point of view of an autocrat with absolute power of life and death, much of it does not bear on the relations among friends, family members, coworkers, or strangers. But several of its central concerns, contained in the excerpts that follow, can speak to people like the author and the readers of this book.

First it confronts an unfortunate fact: while one important way of "doing right by others" is making sure that they receive exactly what they deserve, giving them what they deserve sometimes means giving them what they do not want—a rebuke, a scolding, or some form of punishment. Beyond considering the proper aims of punishment, the essay also draws several important distinctions: between mercy and another Stoic virtue, strictness (*severitas*); and between mercy and two vices (as the Stoics saw them) with which mercy might be confused, pity and forgiveness. Finally, there are two anecdotes that serve as case studies of mercy in action: Seneca uses one of them to illustrate the practical ends that mercy can serve, in "making any house it reaches happy and calm"; the second shows the virtue being pursued as an end in itself, as a form of

22 (1) In [iniuriis] vindicandis haec tria lex secuta est, quae princeps quoque sequi debet: aut ut eum, quem punit, emendet, aut <ut> poena eius ceteros meliores reddat, aut ut sublatis malis securiores ceteri vivant. Ipsos facilius emendabis minore

justice that "reins itself in short of what could deservedly be ordained," in terms readily transferable to our everyday lives.

Seneca explains how Stoic mercy confronts the necessity of punishment in a way that is dispassionate and carefully calibrated: it does not dwell on the past but looks to the future, aiming not at retribution but at improving the wrongdoer or the community at large.

22 (1) In requiting injuries the law pursues these three goals: correcting the person punished, or making all others better people by punishing him,[2] or allowing them to live more securely once bad actors have been removed from their midst. You will more easily correct the wrongdoer with a lesser penalty: people conduct

poena; diligentius enim vivit, cui aliquid integri superest. Nemo dignitati perditae parcit; inpunitatis genus est iam non habere poenae locum. (2) Civitatis autem mores magis corrigit parcitas animadversionum; facit enim consuetudinem peccandi multitudo peccantium, et minus gravis nota est, quam turba damnationum levat, et severitas, quod maximum remedium habet, adsiduitate amittit auctoritatem. . . . 23 (2) In qua civitate raro homines puniuntur, in ea consensus fit innocentiae et indulgetur velut publico bono. Putet se innocentem esse civitas, erit; magis irascetur a communi frugalitate

their lives more carefully when left some-thing whole and unsullied, whereas no one is chary of a self-respect that has been utterly lost. Having nothing that pun-ishment can affect is a kind of impunity. (2) Moreover, a sparing use of punishment does more to correct a community's hab-its, for a multitude of wrongdoers makes wrongdoing a matter of habit: condemna-tions that come thick and fast lessen the stigma of punishment, and strictness, when unrelieved, loses its moral author-ity, which is its most important healing power. . . . 23 (2) In a community where people are rarely punished,[3] innocence comes to enjoy general support and is kindly regarded as a common good. Pro-vided a community thinks of itself as innocent, it will be; it will be more indig-nant at those who depart from the general

desciscentibus, si paucos esse eos viderit. (*On Mercy* 1.22.1–2, 23.2)

3 (1) Et ne forte decipiat nos speciosum clementiae nomen aliquando et in contrarium abducat, videamus, quid sit clementia qualisque sit et quos fines habeat.

Clementia est temperantia animi in potestate ulciscendi vel lenitas superioris adversus inferiorem in constituendis

standard of goodness if it sees that they are few. (*On Mercy* 1.22.1–2, 23.2)

In the context of righteous punishment, mercy emerges, on the one hand, as a version of justice more lenient than the virtue of "strictness," which exacts the fullest form of a deserved punishment, and, on the other hand, as the opposite of cruelty.

3 (1) And lest the fair-seeming name of mercy should at times deceive us and lead us in the opposite direction [i.e., toward some form of vice], let's see what mercy is, what characteristics it has, and what its boundaries are.

Clemency is "the mind's moderation when it has the power to take revenge," or "mildness in a superior toward an inferior in determining punishment." It's

poenis. Plura proponere tutius est, ne una finitio parum rem conprehendat. . . . Itaque dici potest et inclinatio animi ad lenitatem in poena exigenda. (2) Illa finitio contradictiones inveniet, quamvis maxime ad verum accedat, si dixerimus clementiam esse moderationem aliquid ex merita ac debita poena remittentem: reclamabitur nullam virtutem cuiquam minus debito facere. Atqui hoc omnes intellegunt clementiam esse, quae se flectit citra id, quod merito constitui posset.

4 (1) Quid ergo obponitur clementiae? Crudelitas, quae nihil aliud est quam atrocitas animi in exigendis poenis. . . . (3) Illos ergo crudeles vocabo qui puniendi causam habent, modum non habent, sicut

safer to advance several definitions, lest a single definition fall short of covering the matter. . . . Thus it can also be termed "the mind's inclination toward mildness in exacting punishment." (2) The following definition will not cover every case, but it most closely approximates the truth, to wit: "mercy is moderation that diminishes a due and deserved punishment to some degree." Expect an outcry: "No virtue does for anyone less than what is due!" Yet everyone understands that mercy reins itself in short of what could deservedly be ordained.

4 (1) What, then, is the opposite of mercy? Cruelty, which is nothing other than a mind made savage in exacting punishment. . . . (3) I will call "cruel," then, those who have grounds for punishing but set no limit on the punishment, as

in Phalari, quem aiunt non quidem in homines innocentes sed super humanum ac probabilem modum saevisse. Possumus effugere cavillationem et ita finire ut sit crudelitas inclinatio animi ad asperiora. Hanc clementia repellit <et iubet> longius stare a se, nam <cum> severitate illi convenit. (*On Mercy* 2.3.1–2, 4.1, 3)

in the case of Phalaris, who reportedly exercised his savagery, not against innocent men, to be sure, but beyond any limit that a human being could approve.[4] We can avoid quibbling and use this definition: "cruelty is the mind's inclination toward excessive harshness." Clemency rebuffs this quality and compels it to stay far off; for it is with strictness that mercy is in accord [sc. as a virtue]. (*On Mercy* 2.3.1–2, 4.1, 3)

Mercy is also distinct from and superior to pity (*misericordia*, literally "being unhappy at heart") and forgiveness (*ignoscentia*, literally "taking no notice of"). The latter is unacceptable because it involves giving people nothing of what they deserve. The former is unacceptable because it is an emotion that (on the Stoic view) arises from

4 (4) Ad rem pertinet quaerere hoc loco quid sit misericordia, plerique enim ut virtutem eam laudant et bonum hominem vocant misericordem. Et haec vitium animi est. Vtraque circa severitatem circaque clementiam posita sunt, quae vitare debemus; per speciem <enim seve-ritatis in crudelitatem incidimus, per speciem> clementiae in misericordiam. In hoc leviore periculo erratur, sed par error est a vero recedentium. **5** (1) Ergo quem-admodum religio deos colit, superstitio violat, ita clementiam mansuetudinemque omnes boni viri praestabunt, misericor-diam autem vitabunt; est enim vitium pu-silli animi ad speciem alien<orum mal>o-rum succidentis. . . . Misericordia non

muddled thought and does no more good for its object than clear-eyed mercy.

4 (4) At this point it is relevant to ask what pity is; for most people praise it as a virtue and call someone prone to pity a good man. This too is a vice of the mind. Both vices, pity and cruelty, are close to mercy and strictness, and we must avoid them: because it resembles <strictness, we lapse into cruelty, and because it resembles> mercy, we lapse into pity.[5] Erring in the direction of pity entails less risk, but those who fall away from the truth err equally in both cases. **5** (1) Just as religion cherishes the gods, whereas superstition wounds them, so all good people will display mercy and mildness but avoid pity; for it is the fault of a paltry spirit that collapses at the impression of other people's

causam, sed fortunam spectat; clementia rationi accedit.

(2) Scio male audire apud inperitos sectam Stoicorum tamquam duram nimis . . . : obicitur illi, quod sapientem negat misereri, negat ignoscere. Haec, si per se ponantur, invisa sunt; videntur enim nullam relinquere spem humanis erroribus, sed omnia delicta ad poenam deducere. (3) . . . Sed nulla secta benignior leniorque est, nulla amantior hominum et communis boni adtentior, ut propositum sit usui esse et auxilio nec sibi tantum, sed universis singulisque consulere. (4) Misericordia est aegritudo animi ob

<woes>. . . . Pity looks only at the state a person is in, not its cause; mercy is in accord with reason.

(2) I know that the Stoics have a bad reputation among the ignorant for being too callous . . . : they're charged with asserting that the wise man does not feel pity and does not forgive. Taken by itself, that assertion is invidious, for it implies that the Stoics leave human error no hope, but instead refer all shortcomings directly to punishment. (3) . . . But no philosophical school is kinder and gentler, nor more loving of humankind and more attentive to our common good, to the degree that its very purpose is to be useful, bring assistance, and consider the interests not only of its own members but of all people, individually and collectively. (4) Pity is a distress caused by

alienarum miseriarum speciem aut tristitia ex alienis malis contracta, quae accidere inmerentibus credit; aegritudo autem
in sapientem virum non cadit; serena eius
mens est, nec quicquam incidere potest,
quod illam obducat. . . .

6 (1) . . . Tristitia inhabilis est ad dispi-
ciendas res, utilia excogitanda, periculosa
vitanda, aequa aestimanda; ergo non
miseretur, quia id sine miseria animi non
fit. (2) Cetera omnia, quae, qui miseren-
tur, volo facere, libens et altus animo
faciet; succurret alienis lacrimis, non
accedet; dabit manum naufrago, exuli
hospitium, egenti stipem, . . . donabit
lacrimis maternis filium et catenas solvi

the impression of others' unhappiness, or a sadness brought on by the woes of others who one believes are suffering undeservedly.[6] But distress does not visit the wise, whose minds are cheerful, nor can anything happen to them that would bring on distress. . . .

6 (1) . . . Sadness is unsuited to seeing to the heart of things, to figuring out what is helpful, to avoiding risks, and to calculating what is fair. Therefore, the wise will not commiserate, since that necessarily entails the mind's misery. (2) All the other things I think people who feel pity should do, the wise will do gladly and with mind uplifted: they will bring succor to another's tears, not join in them; they will give a hand to the shipwrecked, shelter to the exile, a coin to the needy. . . . They will release a son in answer to a mother's

iubebit et ludo eximet et cadaver etiam
noxium sepeliet, sed faciet ista tranquilla
mente, voltu suo. (3) Ergo non miserebi-
tur sapiens, sed succurret, sed proderit, in
commune auxilium natus ac bonum publicum, ex quo dabit cuique partem. . . .
Quotiens poterit, fortunae intercedet; ubi
enim opibus potius utetur aut viribus,
quam ad restituenda, quae casus inpulit?
Voltum quidem non deiciet nec animum
ob crus alicuius aridum aut pannosam
maciem et innixam baculo senectutem;
ceterum omnibus dignis proderit et

tears and bid his chains be undone; they will free the gladiator from his training; they will bury even a criminal's corpse. But they will do all those things with a tranquil mind and unaltered expression. (3) The wise, then, will not feel pity, but they will give aid and be useful, having been born to assist their fellows and add to the common good, of which they will give each person a share. . . . Whenever possible, they will stand in misfortune's way: for when will they rather use their strength and resources than in restoring what misfortune has overthrown? Surely their expressions will not be downcast, nor their minds either, at the sight of someone's withered leg or people reduced to rags and bone, supporting their old age on a cane; but they will do good for all

deorum more calamitosos propitius respiciet. . . .

7 (1) "At quare non ignoscet?" Agedum constituamus nunc quoque, quid sit venia, et sciemus dari illam a sapiente non debere. Venia est poenae meritae remissio. . . . Ei ignoscitur, qui puniri debuit; sapiens autem nihil facit, quod non debet, nihil praetermittit, quod debet; itaque poenam, quam exigere debet, non donat. (2) Sed illud, quod ex venia consequi vis, honestiore tibi via tribuet; parcet enim sapiens, consulet et corriget. . . . Aliquem verbis tantum admonebit, poena non

who are worthy and, like the gods, look with kindness on those in distress. . . .

7 (1) A question: "But why will they not grant forgiveness?" Very well, let's now also determine what "pardon" is, and we will then understand that a wise man ought not grant it. Pardon is "the remission of a deserved punishment." . . . Forgiveness is granted to one who ought to be punished; the wise, however, neither do anything they ought not do nor forgo doing anything they ought to do. Accordingly, they do not remit a punishment that they ought to exact. (2) But what you want to gain from a pardon the wise will grant you by a more honorable path: for they will spare you, take thought for your real interests, and set you straight.[7] . . . They'll give someone only an admonition and not punish

adficiet aetatem eius emendabilem intu-
ens; aliquem invidia criminis manifeste
laborantem iubebit incolumem esse, quia
deceptus est, quia per vinum labsus;
hostes dimittet salvos, aliquando etiam
laudatos, si honestis causis pro fide, pro
foedere, pro libertate in bellum acciti
sunt.

(3) Haec omnia non veniae, sed clementiae opera sunt. Clementia liberum arbi-
trium habet; non sub formula, sed ex
aequo et bono iudicat; et absolvere illi
licet et, quanti vult, taxare litem. Nihil ex
his facit, tamquam iusto minus fecerit,

him, seeing that he is at a stage in life where he is not yet incorrigible; someone else, who is plainly distressed at the ill will that his crime has incurred, they will tell to depart unscathed, because he was misled or because he slipped while tipsy; they will release enemies unharmed, sometimes even with words of praise, if they were summoned forth to war in an honorable cause, out of loyalty, or in defense of a treaty or their freedom.

(3) All these actions are proper to mercy, not pardon. Mercy exercises freedom of judgment: it makes its determinations not according to a fixed formula but according to what is fair and good; it is free to acquit, and free to assess the value of a suit at the amount it wishes. It does all these things, not as though it were doing less than what is just, but as though the

sed tamquam id, quod constituit, iustissimum sit. Ignoscere autem est, quem
iudices puniendum, non punire; venia
debitae poenae remissio est. Clementia
hoc primum praestat, ut, quos dimittit,
nihil aliud illos pati debuisse pronuntiet;
plenior est quam venia, honestior est.
(*On Mercy* 2.4.4–5.4, 6.1–3, 7.1–3)

determination it reaches is the most just.[8] But to forgive is to forgo punishing one whom you judge ought to be punished, and pardon is the remission of a deserved punishment. Clemency accomplishes this first and foremost: it declares that those whom it lets go ought not to have suffered anything more. Its judgment is more complete than pardon, and more honorable. (*On Mercy* 2.4.4–5.4, 6.1–3, 7.1–3)

Addressing Nero and aiming to make the notion of mercy appealing, Seneca emphasizes the prudential purposes that it can serve, in making the ruler loved rather than feared, and therefore safer on his throne. He uses the example of Caesar Augustus (63 BCE–14 CE), who brought a generation of civil war to an end and ruled Rome's empire

9 (2) Delatum est ad [Augustum] indicium L. Cinnam, stolidi ingenii virum, insidias ei struere; dictum est, et ubi et quando et quemadmodum adgredi vellet; unus ex consciis deferebat. (3) Constituit se ab eo vindicare . . . , nox illi inquieta erat, cum cogitaret adulescentem nobilem, hoc

as its first autocrat for the last forty-five years of his life. Early in his reign, when some thought the idea of one-man rule a repugnant novelty, he was repeatedly the target of would-be assassins, whom he punished when their plans were detected: here Seneca tells the story of the last such attempt on his life, and of the mercy that he showed the culprit, very much to his own advantage.

9 (2) [Augustus] received evidence that Lucius Cinna, a man of no great intelligence, was plotting against him: the where, the when, and the how of the attack were spelled out by one of the conspirators. (3) He decided to take vengeance on Cinna . . . then spent an uneasy night reflecting on the fact that he had to condemn a young man of notable

detracto integrum, Cn. Pompei nepotem, damnandum. . . . (4) Gemens subinde voces varias emittebat et inter se contrarias: "Quid ergo? ego percussorem meum securum ambulare patiar me sollicito? Ergo non dabit poenas, qui tot civilibus bellis frustra petitum caput . . . , postquam terra marique pax parata est, non occidere constituat, sed inmolare?" (nam sacrificantem placuerat adoriri). (5) Rursus silentio interposito maiore multo voce sibi quam Cinnae irascebatur: "Quid vivis, si perire te tam multorum interest? quis finis erit suppliciorum? quis sanguinis? . . . Non est tanti vita, si, ut ego non peream, tam multa perdenda sunt."

family who was thoroughly decent, save for this one incident, and a grandson of Gnaeus Pompey.[9] . . . (4) With a groan he began to muse out loud, his words in conflict with themselves: "What am I to do, then? Am I to let my assassin stroll about without a care while I am wracked by anxiety? Will he not be punished, when he has undertaken not just to kill me but to offer me up as a blood sacrifice" (for Cinna had decided to assail Augustus when he was sacrificing) "after I've survived attacks in so many civil wars . . . ?" (5) But then again, after falling silent, he began to speak much more loudly and in anger, more at himself than at Cinna: "Why live, if so many have an interest in your dying? What end will there be to punishment and to bloodshed? . . . Life is not worth so great a price, if so much

(6) Interpellavit tandem illum Livia uxor et: "Admittis" inquit "muliebre consilium? Fac, quod medici solent, qui, ubi usitata remedia non procedunt, temptant contraria. Severitate nihil adhuc profecisti . . . Nunc tempta, quomodo tibi cedat clementia; ignosce L. Cinnae. Deprensus est; iam nocere tibi non potest, prodesse famae tuae potest."

(7) Gavisus, sibi quod advocatum invenerat, uxori quidem gratias egit, . . . imperavit et Cinnam unum ad se accersit dimissisque omnibus e cubiculo, cum alteram Cinnae poni cathedram iussisset: . . . (8) "Ego te, Cinna, cum in hostium castris invenissem, non factum

destruction is required to prevent my own destruction."

(6) At last his wife, Livia, interrupted him and said: "Will you take a woman's advice? Do what doctors do when the usual prescriptions have no effect: try the opposite remedies. Strictness has gotten you nowhere . . . [she then reels off a string of earlier attempts]. Now try and see how far mercy gets you: let Lucius Cinna go. He's been caught and now can do you no harm, though he can do your reputation some good."

(7) Delighted to have found a counselor, Augustus thanked his wife heartily . . . and summoned Cinna all by himself. Dismissing everyone else from his chamber and ordering that another chair be provided for Cinna, he said: . . . (8) "Cinna, though I found you in the camp of my

tantum mihi inimicum sed natum, ser-
vavi, patrimonium tibi omne concessi.
Hodie tam felix et tam dives es, ut victo
victores invideant. Sacerdotium tibi pe-
tenti praeteritis conpluribus, quorum pa-
rentes mecum militaverant, dedi; cum sic
de te meruerim, occidere me constitu-
isti," (9) . . . adiecit locum, socios, diem,
ordinem insidiarum, cui conmissum esset
ferrum. (10) Et cum defixum videret nec
ex conventione iam, sed ex conscientia
tacentem: "Quo" inquit "hoc animo
facis? ut ipse sis princeps? male mehercules cum populo Romano agitur, si tibi ad
imperandum nihil praeter me obstat. . . .

foes, an enemy born, not made, I let you live and keep your family estate. Today you are so prosperous and wealthy that the victors envy the vanquished. I passed over many whose fathers fought by my side to give you the priesthood you sought. But though I deserved your gratitude, you undertook to kill me," (9) . . . and he specified the place, his co-conspirators, the arrangement of the ambush, and the person entrusted with the weapon. (10) And when he saw that Cinna was thunderstruck and silent . . . from full awareness of what he'd done, Augustus said: "What's your aim in doing this? Do you mean to be prince yourself? My God, the Roman people really are in a bad way if I'm the only thing standing between you and supreme authority! . . . Really, nothing could be easier, you

Adeo nihil facilius potes quam contra Caesarem advocare. Cedo, si spes tuas solus inpedio, Paulusne te et Fabius Maximus et Cossi et Servilii ferent tantumque agmen nobilium non inania nomina praeferentium, sed eorum, qui imaginibus suis decori sint?"

(11) Ne totam eius orationem [sc. repeto] (diutius enim quam duabus horis locutum esse constat, cum hanc poenam, qua sola erat contentus futurus, extenderet): "Vitam" inquit "tibi, Cinna, iterum do, prius hosti, nunc insidiatori ac parricidae. Ex hodierno die inter nos amicitia incipiat; contendamus, utrum ego meliore fide tibi vitam dederim an tu debeas." (12) Post hoc . . . amicissimum

suppose, than to raise a hue and cry against Caesar! Look: if I'm the only obstacle to your hopes, will Paulus and Fabius Maximus and men like Cossus and Servilius[10] put up with you—yes, and the whole great troop of notable men, not the ones who offer nothing but a name, but those who bring honor to their ancestors?"

(11) Not to . . . repeat everything he said (for it's well known that he [scolded Cinna] for more than two hours, drawing out in this way the sole punishment with which he was going to rest content): "I give you your life, Cinna," Augustus said, "for the second time, formerly as my enemy under arms, now as a conspirator and parricide.[11] From this day let our friendship commence, and let us compete to see who acts in better faith—I as your savior, or you as my debtor." (12) After

fidelissimumque habuit. . . . Nullis amplius insidiis ab ullo petitus est. (*On Mercy*
1.9.2–12)

this . . . he had Cinna as his dearest and most loyal friend. . . . Augustus was never again the object of a conspiracy. (*On Mercy* 1.9.2–12)

It must be said that this edifying story—in which Augustus, following Livia's advice, dispenses mercy as a tactical move made to gain an advantage—is not strictly in line with the Stoic principle that though behaving virtuously can be advantageous, one should not choose to behave virtuously for that reason. But Seneca tells another story that very clearly shows the virtue of mercy in action as a thing chosen for its own sake: the story of Augustus, the rich man Tarius, and Tarius's son.

The story involves a core principle of Roman life, and an important institution. The principle is that of "the power of the

father" (*patria potestas*), which held that a father held absolute power—the power of life and death—over all those who were members of his household and subject to his authority: in this respect the household's enslaved members and its free members—the father's children included—stood on an equal footing. In this case, the son had been revealed to be a would-be parricide and so faced the gruesome traditional punishment: being flogged, sewn up in a sack with a rooster, snake, monkey, and dog, and thrown into the sea. Whether he would suffer that punishment would be determined through a traditional institution, the domestic trial: a hearing would be held in the father's home, before an advisory council comprising a number of the father's friends, with the father presiding, and the outcome would be determined by a vote of the

14 (1) [Boni patres] obiurgare liberos non numquam blande, non numquam minaciter solent, aliquando admonere etiam verberibus. Numquid aliquis sanus filium a prima offensa exheredat? Nisi magnae et multae iniuriae patientiam evicerunt, nisi plus est quod timet quam quod damnat, non accedit ad decretorium stilum. Multa ante temptat quibus dubiam indolem et peiore iam loco positam revocet; simul deploratum est, ultima experitur. Nemo ad supplicia exigenda pervenit

council's members, acting as a jury. In this case, the father's friends included Caesar Augustus.

14 (1) [Good fathers] are accustomed to reproving their children, sometimes gently, sometimes menacingly, now and again admonishing them even with blows. No sane man disinherits a son at his first offense, does he? No, he does not take up the pen to draft that decree save when grievous and repeated injuries have overcome his patience, or when the behavior he fears is worse than the behavior he condemns. Before it comes to that he tries many ways to recall a wavering character from its present, regrettable condition; the final steps are taken when hope is lost. No one reaches the point of exacting punishment unless he has tried all possible

nisi qui remedia consumpsit. . . . (3) Tarde sibi pater membra sua abscidat, etiam cum absciderit reponi cupiat et in abscidendo gemat cunctatus multum diuque: prope est enim ut libenter damnet qui cito, prope est ut inique puniat qui nimis.

15 (2) Tarium, qui filium deprensum in parricidii consilio damnavit causa cognita, nemo non suspexit, quod contentus exilio et exilio delicato Massiliae parricidam continuit et annua illi praestitit, quanta praestare integro solebat; haec liberalitas effecit, ut, in qua civitate numquam deest patronus peioribus, nemo

cures. . . . (3) Let a father be slow to amputate his own limbs,[12] let him even, once he has done it, wish them put back in place, and when after long delay he does it, let him groan. For when a person is quick to condemn, it is almost as though he is glad to condemn; excessive punishment is the next thing to unwarranted punishment.[13]

15 (2) When Tarius discovered that his son was planning his death and condemned him in a trial held in his own household, everyone respected him because he was content to sentence the young man to exile—and a pampered exile at that, in Massilia, where he provided him with the same annual allowance he used to give him before his disgrace.[14] Because of this generous gesture everyone

dubitaret, quin reus merito damnatus esset, quem is pater damnare potuisset, qui odisse non poterat.

(3) Hoc ipso exemplo dabo, quem conpares bono patri, bonum principem. Cogniturus de filio Tarius advocavit in consilium Caesarem Augustum; venit in privatos penates, adsedit, pars alieni consilii fuit, non dixit: "Immo in meam domum veniat"; quod si factum esset, Caesaris futura erat cognitio, non patris. (4) Audita causa excussisque omnibus, et his, quae adulescens pro se dixerat, et his, quibus arguebatur, petit, ut sententiam suam quisque scriberet, ne ea omnium

in Rome—where even scoundrels never lack an advocate—believed that the young man had been justly condemned, seeing that a father incapable of hating him had been able to condemn him.

(3) This very same episode also provides a model of the good prince for you to compare with the good father. When Tarius was going to conduct the trial he asked Caesar Augustus to sit on his advisory council; and so Augustus came to a private home and sat at Tarius's side as a counselor—he did not say, "No, no, let him come to *my* home," for in that case the trial would have been Caesar's, not the father's. (4) When the case had been heard and the evidence thoroughly examined—both the points that the young man made on his own behalf and those that tended to convict him—

fieret, quae Caesaris fuisset; deinde, pri-
usquam aperirentur codicilli, iuravit se
Tarii, hominis locupletis, hereditatem non
aditurum. (5) Dicet aliquis: "Pusillo
animo timuit, ne videretur locum spei
suae aperire velle fili damnatione." Ego
contra sentio; quilibet nostrum debuisset
adversus opiniones malignas satis fiduciae
habere in bona conscientia, principes
multa debent etiam famae dare. Iuravit se
non aditurum hereditatem. (6) Tarius
quidem eodem die et alterum heredem
perdidit, sed Caesar libertatem sententiae
suae redemit; et postquam adprobavit

Augustus asked that each man write down his own judgment, lest everyone make Caesar's verdict his own. Then, before the tablets were opened, he took an oath that he had no intention of accepting an inheritance from Tarius, who was a wealthy man.[15] (5) Someone will say, "That was a petty concern, not wanting to seem to make room for himself by voting to condemn the son." Quite the opposite, I think: any of us ordinary folk should have had sufficient confidence in his own clear conscience to withstand malicious talk, but princes must make many concessions even to gossip. He swore that he would not accept an inheritance. (6) And indeed on the same day Tarius lost two heirs,[16] but Caesar secured his own freedom of judgment; and after he proved that his own strictness was

gratuitam esse severitatem suam, quod
principi semper curandum est, dixit rele-
gandum, quo patri videretur. (7) Non
culleum, non serpentes, non carcerem de-
crevit memor, non de quo censeret, sed
cui in consilio esset; mollissimo genere
poenae contentum esse debere patrem
dixit in filio adulescentulo inpulso in id
scelus, in quo se, quod proximum erat ab
innocentia, timide gessisset; debere illum
ab urbe et a parentis oculis submoveri.
(*On Mercy* 1.14.1, 3, 15.2–7)

not self-interested—a prince's constant concern—he said that the son should be banished, the location to be left to the father's discretion. (7) Mindful not of the charge he was judging but of the man he was advising, he decreed neither the sack nor snakes nor a prison cell but made plain that a father should be content with the mildest punishment in the case of a young son driven to a crime in which he had shown himself, by his timid conduct, only one step removed from innocence: he should be removed from the city and from his father's sight. (*On Mercy* 1.14.1, 3, 15.2–7)

As Seneca tells it, the story presents a carefully choreographed display of virtue and tact. Conscious of his authority, Augustus requests a secret ballot, so that his authority

will not distort the process. Conscious of both his son's intended crime and his prior life, the father is bound to impose a punishment but mitigates it on rational grounds that can be clearly stated—the young man was "only one step removed from innocence"—and Augustus concurs in the decision. Both father and emperor arrive at their decisions dispassionately, with their judgment unclouded by the anger or vindictiveness that attempted parricide might ordinarily inspire, but with a mild and humane clarity of mind that makes careful calibration possible: had the son been slightly further removed from innocence, we can infer, the punishment would have been somewhat less gentle, with a less generous allowance supporting him in a less congenial setting. Finally, the story illustrates and vindicates the claim that we saw Seneca make when

distinguishing mercy from strictness on the one hand and from pity or forgiveness on the other:

> Mercy exercises freedom of judgment: it makes its determinations not according to a set formula but according to what is fair and good, . . . [and] not as though it were doing less than what is just, but as though the determination it reaches is the most just.

NOTES

INTRODUCTION

1. A fourth collection, *Natural Questions*, is primarily devoted not to ethics but to what the ancient philosophers called "physics," an understanding of how the natural world is constituted.

2. As we have it, *On Mercy* is incomplete, either because it was damaged in transmission or because Seneca abandoned it, perhaps because he recognized the project's futility.

3. In much the same way, the Romans' various gods—of the sun, moon, wine, and

the rest—can be thought of as the different ways in which the providential God's beneficence is manifested in different circumstances (*On Benefits* 4.7–8). For the most part Seneca uses the singular and plural nouns interchangeably: where "gods" stands in the translation of a given passage, you are free to understand "God."

4. The translations are based on the Latin texts published by Oxford University Press in the Oxford Classical Texts series: for the *Moral Epistles* and *Dialogues*, the editions of L. D. Reynolds, published in 1965 and 1977, respectively; for *On Benefits* and *On Mercy*, my own edition, published in 2022. The translations of passages from *On Anger* and *On Mercy* published here are adapted from my own translations previously published in *Seneca: Anger, Mercy, Revenge*, translated by Robert A. Kaster

and Martha C. Nussbaum (Chicago: University of Chicago Press, © 2010). Reproduced with permission of the University of Chicago Press.

1. Striving for Magnanimity

1. "Magnanimity" is derived from Latin *magnanimitas*, the quality of having a "large (*magnus*) mind (*animus*)"; in what follows I use "large-mindedness" and "magnanimity" interchangeably. The opposite of a *magnus animus* is a *pusillus animus* ("teensy mind"), the source of English "pusillanimity," which tends to be used more narrowly (denoting "cowardice" and the like) than the contrasting virtue.

2. Seneca does not take account of another difference, one conditioned by our mortality: humans live in time, with knowledge

that is limited by time, whereas the mind of God knows, at once, all that has been, is now, and ever will be.

3. "Fortune's gifts" are the "indifferents," as the Stoics called them, things external to the mind that are not needed for the best human life. Some (e.g., wealth, good health) can be "preferred"; others (e.g., poverty, illness) can be "dispreferred"; but all should be regarded with detachment, and none should be thought truly good or bad: see the introduction.

4. A Stoic philosopher whom Seneca knew and respected as a young man.

5. Because it was *nefas*—a sacrilege—for a human being to look upon a divine being.

6. The epithet "younger" is commonly applied to this Cato to distinguish him from his great-grandfather, Cato "the Elder" or "the Censor," one of the most influential Romans of the early second century BCE.

7. Socrates (469–399 BCE) served as a hoplite soldier in the early stages of the Peloponnesian War between Athens and Sparta, which began in 431 and ended with Athens's surrender in April 404. An oligarchy (the "Thirty Tyrants") controlled the city for a year after the defeat; negotiations led to the restoration of a free democratic government in September 403. It was under the democracy that Socrates was tried and executed, hence the reference to "a freedom crueler than war and tyrants."

8. Cato (born 95 BCE) committed suicide in Africa after his army's defeat by Julius Caesar in a key battle of the civil war (April 46); his death became the centerpiece of his legend. Here he is said to have been "stymied" in death because his wound was initially sewn up after he stabbed himself in the abdomen; he subsequently tore open the wound and drew out his entrails.

9. For the consulship, the Rome Republic's most important office, in 52 BCE.

10. The reference to exile is unclear: Seneca probably thinks of the commission Cato accepted to organize the new province of Cyprus in 58–56 BCE, time spent away from the center of political life in Rome that Cicero—for complicated reasons of his own—characterized as a period of "exile" for Cato.

11. The philosopher Epicurus (341–270 BCE) founded the school of thought that bears his name. Pythocles and Idomeneus were members of his circle; he wrote a letter to the latter urging him to withdraw from politics.

12. As in the other epistles, the "you" here is Seneca's friend Lucilius, who had risen to the second rank of Rome's elite, the "knights," wealthy men who did not pursue a career in Rome's Senate, though they commonly served in various administrative

posts, as Lucilius did. They enjoyed certain privileges, including access to the seats in the first fourteen rows of the theater, to which Seneca soon alludes.

2. BEING CALM, THINKING CLEARLY

1. Seneca is speaking of a woman who accompanied his wife when she left her father's household and joined his.

2. Homer *Odyssey* 12.39–54, 158–200: after the sorceress Circe warned Odysseus of the Sirens, who lured sailors to destruction with their song, he ordered his men to stop their ears with softened wax and to bind him to the mast, so that he could safely hear them sing.

3. The quotation alludes to the boast of a ship captain from Rhodes, to the effect that not even the god of the sea could deflect him from skillfully doing his duty.

3. Judging Yourself Fairly

1. "Reception hall": a reference, especially, to the morning greetings (*salutatio*) that a distinguished man's friends and dependents would come to deliver at his home, with the gathering's size providing visible proof of his importance.

2. "Vicissitudes": Seneca alludes to the principle that whenever one person freely bestows a benefit on another, the true benefit consists of the goodwill that prompts the action, whatever the material form the benefit happens to take: the latter can be lost or destroyed, but the intention with which the act was performed remains unchanged.

3. Seneca is thinking of a banquet, an occasion when Romans dined reclining, three to a couch: honor and prestige were encoded in the details of who reclined where.

4. Ennius (239–169 BCE) was the first Roman poet to adopt the dactylic hexameter meter used in Greek epic poetry from Homer on, though by Seneca's day his verse technique was considered a bit unrefined. Hortensius (114–50 BCE) was displaced by Cicero (106–43 BCE) as the foremost orator of their day: the former was known for a florid style that presumably was not to Seneca's liking, while Cicero's poetry was commonly held to be as weak as his oratory was powerful.

4. DOING RIGHT BY OTHERS

1. On the Stoic view, the fact that reason can cause movement and action—when I am faced with a closed door, my reasoning causes me to extend my hand, then grasp and turn the knob—demonstrated that it must be a physical entity.

2. One of the founders of the atomic theory of the universe, Democritus (born around 460 BCE) argued that cultivating cheerfulness should be life's goal. He perhaps came to be contrasted with the earlier philosopher Heraclitus because the latter believed that most people understand very little about life and their own place in the world.

3. Seneca is suggesting ways of thinking that we can adopt to avoid disappointment or envy when a benefactor seems to have let us down.

4. Literally, "the greater city," alluding to the distinction that Stoicism's founder, Zeno (335–263 BCE), drew between the earthly communities in which we live and the universal community that gods and human beings share as rational beings.

5. Seneca alludes to the Stoic view, which he embraced with special fervor, that there are

circumstances in which killing oneself is a rational option.

6. Seneca has in mind a game like volleyball, save that there was no net, and the aim was to pat the ball to the other player, not drive it past him.

7. Seneca is addressing Nero: see the introduction to chapter 5.

8. That is, after a wrongdoer has been punished by being blasted by lightning: such a death placed the deceased beyond ordinary human contact and required that he be buried on the spot, attended to by a special category of priest.

9. On the interchangeable singular and plural forms, see the introduction, note 3.

10. Certain Roman magistrates wore a toga with a purple border along its upper edge.

11. This is the core Stoic principle that all human beings are naturally endowed with the capacity for wisdom; the "labels" that

denote differences of status are not the products of nature.

12. One of Seneca's teachers, Quintus Sextius (late first century BCE — early first century CE) founded a short-lived school of thought that blended Stoicism with elements of other philosophical traditions and emphasized practical ethics.

5. Being Merciful

1. The Latin word *clementia* corresponds closely to two English terms, "mercy" and the word derived from the Latin, "clemency." I use the two interchangeably in this chapter.

2. That is, punishing a bad actor to teach others a morally improving lesson.

3. That is, rarely need to be punished.

4. Phalaris, tyrant of Acragas in Sicily (ruled ca. 570–549 BCE), roasted miscreants alive in a massive bronze bull.

5. At some point a scribe's eye jumped from the first occurrence of the phrase "because it resembles" (*per speciem*, literally "because of [its] appearance") to the second occurrence, with the result that everything in between was omitted. The words in angle brackets here are a supplement first suggested in the late nineteenth century, though the problem was noticed, and corrections were attempted, at least seven centuries earlier.

6. That is, someone feeling pity incorrectly accepts as valid the impression that another person has undeservedly suffered something bad—a loss, an injury, or the like—when in fact the only thing that is truly bad is the absence of virtue, for which no one but oneself can be responsible.

7. This is the intended effect of the scolding that Augustus administers to the would-be assassin Cinna in the next excerpt.

8. This claim will be illustrated and justified by the anecdote with which this chapter ends.

9. Gnaeus Pompey (Pompey the Great) was the enemy of Julius Caesar in the civil war that ended the Roman Republic (49–45 BCE); because Augustus was Caesar's son by adoption, he could regard Pompey as an ancestral enemy, hence his remark further on that this Cinna, whose mother was Pompey's daughter, was "an enemy born, not made." As Augustus also subsequently says, he had already pardoned Cinna once, after he fought on the losing side in another civil war, which ended with the battle of Actium (31 BCE) and confirmed Augustus's autocratic position.

10. Aristocrats of the highest standing, as members of patrician families who became consuls under Augustus.

11. "Parricide" because Augustus was regarded as the "father of the homeland" (*pater patriae*), a title formally bestowed on him in 2 BCE.

12. As "we are God's limbs" (chapter 4, epigraph), children (according to the Roman view) are their father's.

13. Literally "next thing to unjust punishment": but since excessive punishment is itself unjust, Seneca must mean punishment not merited by the facts of the matter.

14. Massilia (modern Marseille), by ancient origin a Greek colony and a place of wealth and culture, was a frequent refuge of Romans in exile.

15. "Tablets": two small, thin rectangles of wood were used, the face of one coated with

wax on which the verdict was inscribed with a stylus before the tablets' faces were brought together and sealed. "Inheritance": members of the Roman elite commonly included legacies for the emperor in their wills, as tokens of esteem and social intimacy; but as the next sentence shows, Augustus's participation in the hearing could lead to a different, invidious interpretation of his inclusion in Tarius's will.

16. Seneca leaves it to be understood that however mildly the son was punished, he was still disinherited.